THE FINE ART OF HYPOCHONDRIA

The Fine Art of Hypochondria

---

or
How Are You?

---

by Goodman Ace
Illustrated by F. B. Modell

DOUBLEDAY & COMPANY, INC.

GARDEN CITY, NEW YORK

1966

TO JANE, who through the years of sleepless nights cooled my fevered brow by reciting "Insomnia is only mind over mattress." And who lulled me into a false euphoria by constantly reminding me that it was better to be well for one year than sick for one day.

Prologue

FOUR pair and seven years ago I became a lifelong, paid-up (and God how I've paid!) member of HA—Hypochondriacs Anonymous. I could have said "paid through the nose" except for an aggravated sinusitis—one of my minor ailments. If, as they say, the business of dying begins when you're born, I've been at it a long, long time. It began when the doctor slapped me on my entrance. As a result I was in bed for a month with a strangulated hernia. And no Blue Cross.

Fellow hypochondriacs will recognize, and empathize with, the multiple symptoms and syndromes with which I did battle down through the years. I come to you with a message of cheer and a *modus vivendi* which will enable you to hope and cope.

This book claims no minor miracle cures. Only major miracle cures. Any hypochondriac worth his palpitations, his dizzy spells, his blurred vision, his retching, his assortment of allergies and of course those old reliable stand-bys, cancer and heart attack, will find the comfort he seeks in the authenticated details scattered through this book by a hypochondriac who has beaten the rap.

It is not intended that the symptoms will vanish. No hypo, first class, can long endure without them. It is the purpose of some of these pages to demonstrate there is an art to handling hypochondria with grace and dignity. Fainting in night clubs, regurgitating in taxicabs, leaning against tall buildings are not accepted *savoir-faire*. I know. I was there, Charlie. I was a mess.

But not now. As note, here am I in complete sanguinity,

writing a book, which will be due last March. Several chapters deal with the art of surviving and functioning despite the myriad of afflictions and the slings and arrows of outrageous antibiotic shots. But most of the chapters demonstrate in gruesome detail the horrendous, everyday traumas that come to a man so beset.

Down through the years my symptoms have persisted but the import and the fears have abated. There are days now when I feel no pain of dread for an entire hour at a time. Which for me is simply super. But that's the way things break for a hypochondriac. This is the year we get Medicare, and all of a sudden, and out of the blue, I feel great.

G. A.

Contents

THE FINE ART OF HYPOCHONDRIA

Who
Am I?

IF you're a hypochondriac, first class, you awaken each morning with the firm resolve not to worry; everything is going to turn out all wrong. I begin the day early collecting injustices. If the elevator doesn't get to me within five seconds after punching the button, I say to the operator when he finally gets there: "I see I missed the nine-thirty elevator." Anything to brighten his day.

Waiting more than thirty seconds for a table in a restaurant is thirty seconds fraught with the most disagreeable, insulting muttering you've ever heard. And the ritual of being admitted to some of the class restaurants has deliciously fed the flame of my hypochondria for many years.

In the caste system of show business along Broadway there are two kinds of nobility—Celebrities and Owls. An Owl is an accomplished actor not too widely known. When his name is mentioned to prospective producers they ask, "Who? Who? Who?" In Manhattan there are also two classes of eating places—restaurants and clubs. In a restaurant you are met by a headwaiter who asks: "How many are you?" In a club you are met by a headwaiter who asks: "Who are you?" If

you have no reservation in a name he can recognize, you are told they are filled up.

About twenty years ago my wife and I were the major stars of a minor radio program broadcast from New York. We were restaurant folk until one evening my wife decided we should try the Stork Club. It was early for dinner but when we got there the rope was up, although the club seemed fairly deserted. I casually held up two fingers as I had often seen William Powell do with Myrna Loy in *The Thin Man* movies.

The man stared coldly and asked if we had reservations.

I confessed we didn't and he replied they were filled up.

Undaunted we tried Club Twenty One. The man there didn't even let us get to the rope. At the door we said we had no reservation, and he said they were all filled up.

Later that evening I learned from Leonard Lyons, the columnist, how the system works. "Did you tell them who you were?" he asked. "No," I replied. "Who am I? I was hungry and I wanted to buy a meal."

About a year after that cataclysmic, ill-starred evening I somehow got on the mailing list of the Stork Club. "Dear Sir," the invitation clanged, "when the dinner bell rings come to the Stork Club. We think we have the finest air conditioned room in town." It was signed Sherman Billingsly, proprietor. I answered it quickly: "Dear S.B.: You THINK you have the finest air conditioned room in town. We know you have. We never received a more frigid reception anywhere."

The following morning, a phone call:

"Hello, is this Mr. Goodman?"

"That's close enough," I replied.

"I'm Mr. Harris at the Stork. You say you were turned down here last night?"

"No, last year."

"Well, Mr. Goodman, did you tell them at the door who you are?"

"Who am I? According to you I'm Mr. Goodman."

"I thought that was Goodman Ace," he said.

"I thought so too."

We finally hung up, both a little confused.

A year or so later a friend, Mervin LeRoy, phoned and announced he and his wife were in town on a visit from Hollywood and would we go with them to the rodeo. I said we would. He asked us to join him at dinner at the Stork Club.

"We don't go to the Stork Club," I told him. "They won't let us in."

"Did you tell them who you are?" he asked.

"No, I never thought of that."

"Well, you should. And besides you can get in with me."

I explained I didn't want to get in with him and we made arrangements to dine separately. We would pick him up in front of the club at 8:15. We drove up at 8:15 and waited. Finally I went in. Two men were guarding the rope.

"Will you tell Mr. LeRoy the car is here?" I said.

"Who's calling for Mr. LeRoy?" one of them asked.

"Mr. Ace."

He disappeared into the club and the other gentleman sidled up to me.

"Is that Mr. Ace of the radio?"

"Yes."

"We haven't seen you in here lately," he said.

"You've never seen me in here. I tried to get in but you wouldn't let me in."

"Did you tell us who you were?"

"No, I don't want to have to tell you who I am."

The other keeper of the rope came panting back.

"Mr. LeRoy," he announced, "wants you and Mrs. Ace to come in and have a drink with him."

"We don't drink in here," I said.

He looked at his partner and at this point they began talking as if I had left the room.

"He said we didn't let him in here one night."

"Did he tell us who he was?"

"He said he doesn't want to have to tell us who he is."

They stared at me briefly and the one who had delivered Mr. LeRoy's invitation said: "Won't you have a drink with Mr. LeRoy? Bert Lahr is with him."

"Bert Lahr can get in here?" I asked. And stalked out.

A month later Jack Benny came into town, phoned and invited me to go to lunch at Twenty One. I explained why I didn't go to Twenty One. Mr. Benny had a novel suggestion. I should have told them who I was.

"And besides," he coaxed, "you can get in with me."

After some haggling it was finally decided I would go if he promised to meet me at the door. I went. He wasn't at the door. But the man was.

"What can I do for you?" he asked.

"I want to see a suit of clothes," I said.

I was about to be turned down when Mr. Benny emerged from the dining room.

"He's with me," he called. He escorted me to the checkroom.

"I'll take your arm," Jack said, "so they'll know you the next time." And he did. And he held my arm again when we finished lunch and walked to the checkroom. A boy in attendance who recognized me from a lesser restaurant said: "Mr. Ace's hat and coat." And as I got into it he said: "Mr. Bernie's hat and coat."

This should be the end of this, but it has a short epilogue. Some years later we were swept into the Stork Club by some visiting celebrity friends and we had dinner with them there several evenings. Anonymously. Gradually we were recognized as regulars. The food was exceptional and we continued having dinner there often. Then for a change we stayed away for about six months, until one night we were with two Owls who asked if we could get into the Stork Club.

"Of course," my wife said. And we went.

Well, what can I tell you? The man at the rope asked if I had a reservation and we didn't have and they were all filled up. We stood around the vestibule watching others come and identify themselves and go in.

There was a phone booth in the lobby. I called the Stork, announced my name and made reservations for four, and ten seconds later ushered my little group up to the rope.

"Do you have a reservation?" the man asked.

"Yes, Ace."

He looked at his sheet.

"Oh yes," he said. "Right this way, Mr. Goodman."

Art of
Hypochondria

I DIDN'T become a hypochondriac until late in my middle twenty-five years—if you will fantasize along with me that a man's life span is seventy-five and is divided into three equal spans of twenty-five.

By the time I was forty I was an apprentice hypochondriac and by the time I reached forty-two, full-blown. At the age of fifty-two I stopped fighting it, accepted senescence as a way of life, and now, some years later, I come to fellow sufferers with the happy report that I still have my marble. Singular.

My symptoms were simple, really, and will no doubt find identification in many hypochondriacal minds. At any given moment and all through any day or night

I could develop a rapid heartbeat and pulse that triggered a shortness of breath accompanied by a fear of dying. It was not so much the actual fear of dying as it was doing it unattractively; lying prone on a strange, busy street somewhere or slumped in a theater seat, or in a restaurant or a crowded elevator, in the home of friends, on a beach or in the snow, in a radio studio or in a strange doctor's office.

Medical schools weren't turning out doctors fast enough for me. Most of the doctors to whom I came crawling for help curtly told me after thorough examinations that there was nothing wrong with me. I made short shrift of them. But I do remember three of my early doctors fondly and with reverence. Of all the medicos to whose offices I beat paths in those years, they were the most patient, they were kindly, and they were always in attendance when needed. They at least satisfied my need for knowing that something was really wrong by separately diagnosing my case as neurocirculatory aesthenia.

Whatever all that meant, at least I had something to go on. It's no picnic having something physically wrong with you and not having a name for it. So I could be found any day in the respective offices of these three doctors. To these three learned men of medicine I will forever be grateful: Dr. Jack Weiner, Dr. Joseph Diamond, and Dr. Foster Kennedy, who, at their untimely passing, I felt were somehow in violation of their Hippocratic oath.

Meanwhile I struggled on with neurocirculatory aesthenia as best I could. When friends met me on the

street and casually asked, "How are you?" I knew they meant: "You look terrible." If somebody remarked, "Haven't seen you in a long time," I knew it was "What hospital have you been in?" I began to find reasons for not going out. I began lying down a lot. As an excuse, I was once in bed for nine days with a bad haircut.

What I needed was some new doctors. I found them.

Shortly thereafter, I found myself in the office of one of the new doctors. He listened raptly to my heart as his feet danced a fast tango to its beat. For fear he might dismiss me as having nothing wrong, I confided that what I had was neurocirculatory aesthenia. To my delight he nodded his head. The symptoms, he told me, were a rapid heartbeat and pulse.

I asked if he could give me something for it. He wrote a prescription. I stuck it in my pocket and walked out. At the first drugstore, I approached the pharmacist, took the prescription out, and was about to hand it to him when I read what the doctor had written:

"You have no organic abnormality of the heart, no feeling of breathlessness is dangerous, nothing bad will happen to you." And he had the nerve to sign it. I tore it to shreds and ordered a tube of toothpaste—small size. I knew now I wasn't going to last long.

What's
Old?

I RUN into a lot of people who say they were in their
doctors' offices the other day and while waiting they
picked up a copy of *Saturday Review* and read this or
that column of mine. Of course that's one way to sub-
scribe to the *Saturday Review*, the cowardly way.

The courageous way is to send a check to the sub-
scription department. At least you would be a little
more *au courant*. One doctor's patient told he he just
read my piece on Adlai Stevenson's poignant concession speech to Dwight Eisenhower. Which will give
you some kind of a musty hint about his doctor's office.
Also about his doctor, who doubtless prescribes Vase-

line for everything and has a goodly store of leeches on hand.

The classic joke about a doctor's office used to be old copies of *National Geographic*. More modern doctors display something a little livelier. My doctor has some old copies of *Time*. Also *Life*. This cheers me. After all, that's what I came looking for in my doctor's office —a little more time, a little more life. And as I sat there wondering what he had discovered during a recent checkup—whether to operate or just touch up the X rays—my eye fell on a stack of pamphlets on a window ledge. They were printed by the Wilson Research Foundation and were titled *The Complete Woman*. Well, the complete woman was also something I had been looking for. But I had never thought to look in a doctor's office. So, with great eagerness, I began reading:

"There were very few old women in the Roman Empire. Life expectancy was about 23 years. At the turn of the century it had risen to 48 years. And there has been recently a marked increase in life expectancy for the woman. A boy born today can expect to live to 68.5 years. A girl, 75.1 years."

Since I was born a boy I began to worry. I wondered why we had been shortchanged like that. It seemed totally unfair. Who made up that rule? Who is this Wilson Research Foundation who gives me 68.5 years and my wife 75.1? I have enough trouble with the Nielsen ratings. Now I have something else to worry about.

"The civilized world is becoming full of women past fifty."

Yes, but try to find one who'll admit being past fifty.

"Such women were once considered old."

Only by women. There are men who consider them old at nineteen.

"However, a large part of their lives is still ahead of them. Many women will live into their eighties or longer."

I threw the pamphlet back on the window ledge and asked the nurse in attendance for a tranquilizer. She said she couldn't give it to me without a prescription. Little did she care about me. She was born a girl. She knew she was going to reach eighty in about fifty years.

Like all good nurses, she thought to calm me and get rid of whatever was troubling my mind by suggesting: "The doctor will be another half hour. Why don't you take a walk—stretch your legs?" Well, there was therapy I hadn't counted on. I always stretch my legs when I walk. It was my years I was interested in stretching. But I hadn't eaten anything that morning so I walked over to a restaurant and made short Schrafft of breakfast.

When I returned, there were two middle-aged ladies now seated in the doctor's office. They stared at me and I at them. They outstared me. I thought they looked disgustingly smug with their eighty-year expectancy while I sat there uncomfortably with my 68.5 showing all over the place.

Then it suddenly dawned on me. It's true! When I

read the obituary page of the *Times* I never see any
women's names or pictures. They must have some secret formula men don't know about. Maybe it's because
they keep themselves in good shape with all those ex-
ercises they are constantly taking—teasing their hair
by the hour (that's pretty strenuous) and holding that
telephone receiver to the ear interminably (that
strengthens the arm and mouth muscles). The only
thing men do is get out there every day and push people around and get pushed around themselves, toting
that barge and lifting that bale, trying to keep up the
payments on those life insurance policies we 68.5's are
going to leave to our 75.1's.

Well, why not? At any age the ladies *are* delightful,
delectable and, most important, deductible. On the
other side of the coin this mournful "September Song"
attitude I have toward growing old is as nothing compared to the threnetic melody of "Think Young" which
I ran into one day in the office of a TV executive. I had
an idea which I hoped to sell him. Doesn't everybody? Hardly a week passes, for example, that I don't
get a letter from a nonprofessional writer who is an
unhappy television viewer and who feels he can do
better with half his brain tied behind his back, and he
has an idea for a situation comedy program and where
does he go and whom does he see? Also, now and
then, a letter from a professional writer who feels he
can do better with his whole brain tied behind his back
and where does he go and whom does he see?

Well, I can tell him whom to see. They'll tell him

where to go. I know a professional writer who wrote for radio for more than twenty years and for television for about fifteen years and he had an idea for a fresh, new-type situation TV comedy and they told *me* where to go.

This has been the fall, winter, and spring of my discontent. And it looks like summer, too. As a graduate of the College of Hard Knocks, *cum stupid*, I was under the delusion that once I walked into any producer's office with a complete outline of this idea with full descriptions of locale, characters, and the flavor of the show I would be accorded the same treatment All-State gives its policyholders—you know, where they hand you the check before you are actually run over or burned out of house and home.

I was living in a fool's paradise. Nothing happens that quickly in television. But not without cause. You see, the first step in launching any new program is to make a pilot of the script. This filmed version of the first episode costs a lot of money. A hundred thousand dollars. So you can hardly fault them for being careful and for asking questions. Which one executive did. And I quote:

"Who is the main character in your show?"

"Well, he's a man about sixty or sixty-five and he owns a—"

"Can't he be younger?"

"Beg pardon?"

"Can't he be younger than sixty?"

"But I haven't told you what he owns."

"That doesn't matter. After a lot of research in depth with charts and graphs and logarithmic calculations we have found that the acceptable age for a leading television personality is thirty-five or under."

By now my hypochondria was going full blast. I knew I should get out of there right away, but I also majored in masochism. So I stayed for the dialogue.

"Thirty-five or under?" I said. "Does Walter Brennan know about this?"

"Oh, is that who you're thinking of, Walter Brennan? Get him. Good!"

"What happened to thirty-five?"

"Well, if it's Walter Brennan, he'll get you the rating. You know what the magic number is now?"

"Thirty-five?"

"No, four."

"You're kidding."

"No, four dollars per thousand."

"You mean four dollars for a thousand scripts?"

"No! A sponsor should get at least a thousand viewers for every four dollars he spends on a TV program. If the rating on your show proves that you have twenty million viewers, that's twenty thousand thousand, and at four dollars per thousand the sponsor is willing to pay eighty thousand dollars."

"Oh, I don't expect to get eighty thousand dollars for writing this script."

"Believe me, you won't. Now what is your show about?"

"Well, I hope it's about a twenty-million-viewer show, but I can't promise that it'll be exactly the—"

"No, no, I mean what's the idea of your show?"

"Oh, you mean writing-wise, not rating-wise. Well, this leading character is about sixty or sixty-five and he owns a—"

"Have you ever watched the Patty Duke show?"

"Well, yes, I did, but I don't see what—"

"Now take Patty Duke."

"I tried—honestly, I tried. I just can't."

"But that show appeals to the teen-age group. They control the TV sets. That's what we're after."

"Oh, then you're not figuring on a cigarette sponsor for my show."

"No, no. We're staying away from cigarettes for teen-agers."

"Well, I could make this character a tobacco-chewer. I haven't seen anything against chewing tobacco."

"You see, we're poles apart. You're talking about the tobacco-chewing set and I'm talking about the bubble-gum set. How about integrating some young people into your show?"

"Well, I don't know. You see this man owns a—"

"You think about it. Good! This has been a most productive meeting. Drop in any time."

Even if I can't take Patty Duke, I can take pills and this time I gulped several of my forgetting tablets. They're not the ones I forget; they're pills to help you forget.

Dialogue
in a Taxi

AFTER one of my annual checkups I stood in the rain in front of my doctor's office. The cab drew up to the curb to unload a lady complete with shopping bag, something wrapped in a newspaper, a large empty picture frame, and, of course, the black leather pocketbook. As the driver pulled the flag, the lady suddenly became aware she would have to pay for the trip.

There followed a shifting of packages until she opened the black leather pocketbook. After some search and some dialogue, which I could not hear because of the rain's beating a sharp tattoo on my tin ear, she went through the black leather pocketbook again and came up with the small change purse. There was a pause for small change identification, and, with the aid of an abacus, a lengthy counting out of small change, more dialogue, and the transaction was finally consummated.

Now she snapped the change purse shut and put it back in the black leather pocketbook along with several tissues that had escaped during the deal, folding each tissue carefully. Following which, there was a reshuffling of the packages; then, opening the taxi door, she hoisted herself out into the rain, holding aloft the empty picture frame so that for one brief instant I was a portrait of "Wet Man Waiting in Rain for Woman to Pay Fare and Get Out So He Can Get In."

As we pulled away, the driver had one succinct comment. "Women!" I couldn't have phrased it better myself. I intoned a reverent amen. "Women," he continued, "they're all alike. First she asks me if I got change for a ten-spot. When I tell her no, she gets mad. I tell her, 'This ain't a bank, lady. I just started hacking.' So she looks through her purse for the change—forty-five cents. Then she says, will I take pennies. Women!"

"I suppose there was no tip," I said.

"Tip?" he shouted. "I was glad to get rid of her. She even give me three pennies instead of five. Women! They're all alike."

I clucked sympathetically, asked him to take me to Penn Station, and we drove in silence. As we skittered down Seventh Avenue, a chauffeur in a limousine cut in on us. Having started the day a two cents loser with his first fare, my man was in no mood to be cut in on.

"Those goddam niggers—they're all alike," he said.

"Yeh?" I said. "How about Jackie Robinson?"

"Yeh, him, too."

"How about Ralph Bunche?"

"Who?"

"I don't think you ought to blame a whole race on what one man does, do you?"

"Ah, they're alike," he said: "Look at all· them street demonstrations, and them marches, and all that."

"Well, they want equal rights."

"That's what I mean."

"Equal opportunities, equal pay."

"Yeh—yeh—all that—that's what I'm talking about."

"What minority group do you belong to?" I asked.

"I don't belong to nothing."

"Everybody belongs. I feel strongly about this matter because my sister happens to be married to a Negro."

"Yeh?" He turned around to look over what he had picked up. This was going to be one of those days.

"That's right," I said. "But he converted. He attends the synagogue every week. When was the last time you were in a synagogue?"

"On the high holidays," he said. "I go once a year."

"You know something?" I replied. "Since you both have the same faith, I think my brother-in-law is a better man than you are."

That was the *coup de pied*. First a woman who short-changed him two cents and now a Negro-lover. He pulled over to the curb. We were a block from Penn Station.

"Get out of my cab," he said.

"Oh no," I demurred. "You have to take me where I'm going."

He pulled the flag. "Get out of the cab."

"If you don't take me, I'll call a cop."

"Call him. I don't care."

"There's one over there," I pointed. And over there, directing traffic, stood a husky Negro traffic cop.

The cabbie drove me into the station. The meter said seventy cents. I gave him two dollars.

"You can keep that," I said. "I'm sorry I gave you a hard time, but you shouldn't blame a whole race on what one member of that race does."

He felt a little expansive with the dollar-thirty tip.

"Yeh, I guess you're right," he replied. "There's good and there's bad."

"Now you're getting it," I said. "And now I'll tell you something. My sister isn't really married to a Negro."

"No?"

"No. It's worse than that. She's forty-six and not married at all."

"Well," he said as he pulled away, "it's better than being married to a goddam nigger."

Lost—a dollar-thirty and one small crusade.

How to
Get By on
$10,000 a Week

NEWSPAPER television critics seem to have a morbid and unfriendly preoccupation with money. "Is it true," they invariably ask, "that you get ten thousand dollars a week for writing that program?" And in their eyes you read the rest of the question: ". . . And they're not eating in Cambodia?" One interviewer snidely asked, "Does it really take five people to write the Perry Como show?" The question, of course, was well put when you consider that a good hunk of the writing consists of "And now in a gayer mood we take you to Latin America, where we hear the rhythmic beat of the Bossa Nova." I took the fellow aside and whispered that it didn't really take five writers and prevailed on him to

keep it confidential, the unemployment rate being what
it is.

Clippings from over the country come to this desk
and, as I swim through this Sargasso Sea of TV critique
of our program last week, I notice that with some cleverly conceived convolutions the writer always winds
up with the money question. Harriet Van Horne, who
writes a distinguished column for the New York
World-Telegram & Sun, did it most gently: "Surely television's highest-paid writer could have come up with
a better finish for the sketch." There is, of course, an
assumption here that the same finish would have
seemed better if the writer hadn't been paid so much.

This roundelay of invective goes on season through
season. It reached a climax recently when even Jane
timidly asked: "Dear, can't you take a job for five thousand a week like everybody else?"

Opening the trap of her hermetically sealed incuba-
tor, I explained why I couldn't afford it. Writing for
television is not all writing. Taking a paycheck, let us
say, of ten thousand dollars a week, I ran down the list
of nondeductible tangible intangibles. First, writing for
a medium in which Batman could be No. 1, there is an
immediate loss of dignity. That averages out to $1,655
a week. And when you lose your dignity there quickly
follows a loss of integrity. My integrity I calculate at
$22.80.

Then there is the business of coaching, coaxing, and
coercing the Star for whom you write. Coaching consists of line readings. For instance, one week there was

the line: "Between you and me." And that's the way
it was printed on the cue card. On the air the Star read
the line: "Between you and I." Without mentioning it
to the Star, I inserted the same line the following week.
Again it came out: "Between you and I." The third
week I had him. The line now read "Strictly between
us." The Star read it: "Strictly between you and I." For
coaching: $880.40.

Coaxing the Star to do the material is a matter of
appealing to his courage to read a line that he thinks
may reflect on his taking sides in a social problem. In a
script there was the character of a United Nations delegate from a mythical country. The straight man said:
"You speak good English. Where did you go to school?"
The delegate replied: "Oxford." The straight man said:
"Oh, England?" And the delegate replied: "Not Missis-
sippi." The Star confided his feeling that we were treating the subject too lightly. After some beseeching and
demonstrating that humor often points up human frail-
ties as well as a seriously written editorial, the line was
left in. The audience not only laughed but applauded
the slight comment. Coaxing, $1,945.15.

Coercing a Star has to do with his opinion that, while
he understands the line, his audience will not get it.
Once I was on a program for which I was being most
highly paid, for we were to have as a guest Bob Crosby.
In planning the script the writing staff decided it would
be a novelty if we didn't mention his brother Bing. So
we did it obliquely. The opening scene was Bob Crosby
on the phone talking to the Star. "Hello," said Bob

Crosby, "this is Bob Crosby." And the Star replied: "Hello, Bob, how's everything in Hollywood?" And Bob Crosby replied: "He's fine." It took a week's rehearsal to convince the Star and Bob Crosby that the line should not be "Bing's fine." Coercing, $1,225.30.

Without going into other details, there are also the matters of convincing a network official that the entendre is not double; of convincing a sponsor you intend no conflict of interest when you write "It's a lucky day for me" on a Camel program; and the important item known as the rating, better known in medical circles as the Nielsen syndrome. It is a scientific fact that the writer's blood pressure runs counterclockwise to the rating his show gets. When the rating drops, his blood pressure goes up. Thus, the doctor gets his share of the loot.

In detail now:

Dignity	$1,655.00
Integrity	22.80
Coaching	880.40
Coaxing	1,945.15
Coercing	1,225.30
Network	1,190.25
Sponsor	965.30
Doctor	2,099.40
TOTAL	9,983.60

So the actual writing of the program comes to $16.40.

But the whole thing is academic. I am presently unemployed.

Only
Sick People Go to
Doctors

I CONTINUE with the proposition that I can cure your hypochondria or at least demonstrate a dignified way of living with it. And I will brook no criticism—clinical or lay, AMA or Walgreen's—in my prescription for a short cut to getting rid of it simply by pointing up the kinship of identical symptoms and discomfitures and treating each with reverence and disdain. This is no more disquieting than your doctor's telling you, as my doctor did, that you are sound as a dollar, when you and de Gaulle know how sound the dollar really is.

One would think that after I had come safely through the years of physical and mental wear and tear of hypochondria I would now, twelve years later, be in gruesome disrepair. *Au contraire!* Physically I may be slightly impaired—those constant treks to doctors' offices can take their toll. But I'm all there mentally, having even developed at this late stage a remarkable total recall.

How about that for a new way of life—a *modus vivendi*—or, I should say, a *modus vivendi passato*. I can recall on a large screen and in color the slightest incident of the past, going as far back as those wonderful childhood days of yesteryear. It's the yesterdays I have most trouble with.

First you must understand that in treating hypochondria a physician is really helpless. There is nothing on which he can put his finger, like a pulse, or a doorbell. We have miracle drugs but we don't have miracle doctors. If you wander into a doctor's office with a series of intangible symptoms, he secretly wishes you had come in with a bad cough, which, as everyone knows, can be cured by a doctor in two weeks or without a doctor by lying abed fourteen days. A rule of thumb in the matter of medical advice is to take everything any doctor says with a grain of aspirin.

I cite case histories—mine. One doctor prescribed walking. "Walk to work every morning," he said. I did. My symptoms continued. True, my office is across the street from where I live. I hope he doesn't read this book.

Another doctor once fluoroscoped my heart and described it as "long and narrow." (That was the style they were wearing those days. Today I understand it's more heart-shaped.) In an attempt to mollify my fears

he said: "If all the ailments in the world were hung out on a line to dry, you would choose your own." That miserable metaphoric prescription was no help. Actually he was wrong. I would have chosen lobar pneumonia compounded with a touch of pleurisy. That he could have handled.

One midnight when I realized I had cancer of the throat, a doctor came in answer to my emergency call and wiped it away with a piece of cotton on the end of a swab stick. Then he said, "Fill your tonsillectomy bag with ice and put it around your throat."

"Tonsillectomy bag?" I asked.

"You mean you don't have one?" he demanded.

I explained I didn't have room in my medicine cabinet for one, and he suggested warm drinks—some hot water with raspberry jam to make it palatable.

"Raspberry jam?" I asked.

Impatiently he went to the refrigerator and vainly searched for raspberry jam. If there was anyone not remotely prepared for this emergency it was I. He finally settled for grape jelly and had some on a slice of white bread.

Another one of my many doctors hit upon a plan. He said it was probably my teeth. I had been so busy being sick I hadn't been to a dentist in some time. I found a good one. He offered to rehabilitate my bite and promised a lifetime job; cost, thirty-five hundred dollars. It was worth it. I didn't feel much better, but I bit a lot better.

Two years later the rehabilitation started to fall apart. Back to the dentist.

"What happened to this lifetime job?" I sarcastically asked.

"Who knew you were going to live this long?" he replied petulantly.

Situation
Comedy

IN my delicate, hypochondriacal, and hypersensitive
condition I can't read a newspaper story without nervously wondering what the "real" story is. I keep reading between the lies. So when some time ago New
York's then-Mayor Wagner and his attractive bride-to-
be announced in a joint statement that when they were
married they would NOT set up housekeeping in the
mayor's official residence, Gracie Mansion, I thought:
"Oh boy, here they go."

The excuse they gave was that since the mayor's
term had only a few months to run, they had both
happily decided that the mayor would move out of
Gracie Mansion and into a Manhattan apartment. Be-

ing a married man I know that such monumental decisions are not so glibly come by. I wonder how it really went?

"OK, Barbara, then if we get married on July 26th that'll give us August, September, October, November, and December—five months in Gracie Mansion before my term is ended."

"Wait a minute—who's moving into Gracie Mansion?"

"You and I. I'm the mayor and I live in Gracie Mansion. You go where your husband goes."

"Hold it Buster—Bob—where did you get the idea we're going to live in the Mansion?"

"Well, I just took it for granted."

"Oh, that's cozy. Already you're taking me for granted."

"Oh no, dear, I mean it's Gracie Mansion—it's expected we live there. And it's five months rent free. You can't get a better rent concession than that. Ask my housing commissioner."

"Your housing commissioner doesn't have to put up new drapes and then tear them down after five months."

"But what's the price of a set of drapes compared to the money we save on five months' free rent?"

"You're a fine one to start talking about saving money. Where were you when the budget came around?"

"Now let's not get personal, Barbara. And besides, you won't have to worry about fixing up Gracie Mansion. I'll get a decorator to do anything you want in the house plus landscaping."

"Yeh? Who you gonna get, Bob Moses? And have him build a bridge across our living room? No thanks."

"It's not only the money we save. Because I'm not exactly slow with a buck. I spend pretty good."

"Yes, so I've heard."

"Where do you think that engagement ring came from? You think I found that in a crackerjack box?"

"I meant to ask you. Where *did* you find it?"

"Very funny. Look, honey, living in Gracie Mansion is tradition. I had a poll taken where we should live. Eighty-two per cent said Gracie Mansion. You know we have to go along with the consensus."

"That's not the consensus in my beauty shop."

"I'm not interested in the girls in your beauty shop! What do they know about politics?"

"Hold the phone—just a minute. Do you think of our marriage as part of those wild campaigns you're putting on to beat that handsome John Lindsay?"

"Well, I don't know about that. Handsome is as handsome does. This is no beauty contest. It's disgraceful the way Lindsay runs around every weekend on those beaches with his shirttail hanging out."

"It's better than your Screvane spending his weekends eating all those messy hot dogs and knishes and pizzas and—"

"We're talking about Gracie Mansion."

"So am I. I don't like it. I have a lovely place picked

out where we're going to live near Gracie Mansion."

"Where's that?"

"It's a half mile just outside Albany."

"I don't want to live outside Albany!"

"Bob, don't you think moving right into Albany would be a little pushy? Let's take it easy."

"This is ridiculous. Look, darling—"

"Or maybe you'd prefer Washington. I saw a beautiful little home there. Just a short trip to the capitol. It's an ideal spot. The kitchen needs a little fixing up. I'll get a cabinetmaker."

"You're talking like a Cabinetmaker! Look, we're both adults. Let's try for a compromise. I don't want to have to call in Arthur Goldberg to negotiate."

"OK, we'll compromise. If you want to live in Gracie Mansion, you live there. I'll move into the place I've picked out and wait for you."

"You must be kidding! Do you realize what the *Times* would say?"

"Darling, I'm only interested in *our* times."

"OK, I give up. You're tougher to deal with than Bobby Kennedy. But you're prettier. You win."

"Oh thank you, dear. You won't change your mind now like you did on the city sales tax."

"I *said* OK."

"OK what? Say it."

"Say what?"

"You know what."

"Oh, all right—good night, Gracie!"

The
Curtain Slowly
Descends

July 17, 1965.
IT has just begun to sink in. Judy Holliday is dead. At
a time like this what good is it being a writer? Here I
sit before a machine with a handful of alphabet staring
up at me and the only words that seem to form are
sorry, loss, solace, and all those futile clichés that go
with messages of condolence.

My acquaintance with this finest and most sensitive
of the theater's comediennes began some fifteen years
ago when I was writing the "Big Show," starring
Tallulah Bankhead, radio's last gasp before the on-
slaught of television. This hour-and-a-half big-name
presentation was a weekly series on NBC, and each

show found its guest list peopled with six or seven of the most glamorous names in entertainment. So it was only natural that Judy should have been one of our earliest guests after her triumph as Billie Dawn in *Born Yesterday*. She did a scene from Garson Kanin's comedy hit and of course she was perfection. But it was in the dialogue that followed, attendant to some chatting our guests always did with Miss Bankhead, that I began to realize that this dumb blonde, Billie Dawn, was the very antithesis of this brilliant woman, Judy Holliday.

Judy was a worrisome girl. She read each line we wrote for her on that first show, and for the many subsequent shows to which she was invited back, with a keen and searching mind, arguing whether a line fit the character she played, whether the comedic line was properly motivated by the straight line. She gave us hours of rewrite and re-rewrite, until she was contented with what she had to speak. But with Judy it was for me always a labor of love. We knew we would always get a bright and shining performance—an understanding reading filled with shadings and nuances and a delivery that was timed to the split second for the audience response we were seeking.

The character we developed for her on that first show was in the mold of Billie Dawn, naturally. She was to be a little suspicious of the glamorous Miss Bankhead—a little timid yet still ready to grapple with this formidable and unpredictable figure.

"A superb characterization, Judy," Miss Bankhead said when the scene from the play had ended. "Come on over and let's chat."

And Judy, looking her over carefully, said: "About what?"

"Why Judy, whenever an actress comes on our show we always have to talk."

"Why?"

"People expect it. This is the 'Big Show.'"

"No wonder you're here for an hour and a half. If you didn't talk so much you could be home in a half hour like everybody else."

And so on.

The Holliday trademark was on every line. Just as it was in the excerpt from *Born Yesterday,* which she performed for us that night. It was the scene with the newspaperman who has been hired by Judy's gauche husband to make a soft and well-spoken lady of her. This is their first meeting, and he says, "Billie—that's a sort of an odd name, isn't it?"

"What are you talkin'? Half the kids I know are named it. Anyway, it's not my real name."

"What is?"

"Holy smoke! Emma."

"What's the matter?"

"Do I look like an Emma?"

"No, you don't look like a Billie, either."

"So what do I look like?"

"You look like a delightful girl."

(*Pause.*)

"Lemme ask you, are you one of them talkers or would you be innarested in a little action?"

A line still quoted fifteen years later.

And yet—and when I say this I genuflect admiringly in the direction of the brilliant Garson Kanin and the genius of his playwriting from title to final curtain—and yet, even in print these lines hold the magic of Judy; one still hears her voice, her inflections, her own personal idiom.

Three years ago I was writing an hour special for her on television. From the start she was intrigued with the concept. She laughed aloud at the comedy lines when she first read the script. Then one day she phoned me. Her agile mind had been at work picking out little things here and there, phrasing, reconstructing, timing, wondering if the character's reactions were true. I said, "Judy, the trouble with you is you ask too many logical questions." She asked if we could meet later in the day to discuss it. I agreed.

While I waited for her in the lobby of my hotel, I thought we'd go to a quiet spot in some elegant restaurant and over a cup of coffee come to some sort of compromise. She showed up in the lobby wearing some tight-fitting jeans, sneakers, her hair in disarray, and wearing a catcher's mitt. She had been playing ball with her son in the park. The restaurant bit was out. We went to my office, where we made some minor changes. The next day the show went on the air.

The morning after the show the reviews came out.

They were divided. But two of the local critics had said, "Too bad Miss Holliday couldn't rise above the material." That evening I found in the box at the hotel a note delivered by hand by Miss Holliday. I've never disclosed this before. I've never shown it to the critics or to anyone else. This is the note:

Dear Goody:

I had to tell you that I thought the reviews with the exception of the *Times* and *Telegram* were most unfair. I know it's traditional to blame the writing. It's almost a reflex action. But in this case it was unwarranted and unjust. I thought the material was excellent. The fault, I'm sorry to say, lay with the performance. I just didn't go that extra step to mastery. Love,

Judy.

Suddenly, midway through life, she's gone. And from the depth of our loss we, like Judy, ask one logical question. Why?

In
the Bad Old
Summertime

THIS was a time in recent summers when we New Yorkers got long-distance phone calls from friends who would say they were coming to see the World's Fair. And a gay, carefree lot they were.

That they haven't written or phoned in some ten years seems to bother them not at all. Their voices teeming with excitement, they would shout: "How are you?" This is immediately followed by the ever popular "Long time no see!" That does it for me. When someone asks a hypochondriac how he is and doesn't give him a chance to state full particulars, he's had it.

This time I murmured something about long time no

letter, birthday card, Christmas greeting, or get-well note.

"You sound great!" one home towner said. "By the way, we're coming to New York to take in the World's Fair. I wonder if you could do me a little favor."

That's where I cut in:

"No, I'm sorry. I can't get you two tickets to *Hello, Dolly!* and I can't get you two tickets to *Fiddler on the Roof* and I can't get you two tickets to *The Odd Couple.*"

There was always a short pause.

"How did you know I was going to ask you that?" he asked.

"Just lucky, I guess."

"Well, you're wrong. We wanted four tickets to *The Odd Couple!*"

I patiently explained that *The Odd Couple* was such a big hit they were selling tickets months in advance.

"You sure of that?" he said. "Because I called the box office several weeks ago and the operator told me the phone was temporarily disconnected. If they're doing that good how come they can't pay their phone bills?"

The phone had been temporarily disconnected when the play first opened because, what with the lines at the box office and the phone calls, the ticket sellers were going slightly berserk. In similar danger myself, I avoided answering.

"Well, how about four to *Hello, Dolly!* Is Carol Burnett still playing in that one?"

"No, Carol Burnett is not playing in *Hello, Dolly!*"

"Well, we wouldn't want to see it without Carol Burnett. That's out. Besides, Helen has her mind made up to see *The Odd Couple*. You sure you can't do anything about it?"

"About Helen's mind? No, I can't."

"I thought you had influence."

"Oh, I have," I said, wanting to save face with the folks back home. "How about some other show?"

"Yeh? Like what?"

"Well—*Do I Hear a Waltz?*"

"No, that's Elaine playing her records."

"Elaine? Who's Elaine?"

"You remember Elaine. Our little girl—she's eight years old now."

Since I hadn't heard from him in ten years, I didn't know there had been an Elaine. Mathematically that works out, doesn't it? But mathematics means nothing to him. Neither does time. Nor does space in a hotel room, which he also asked for. He'd also read somewhere that you can get tickets to hit shows if you buy them in large blocks.

"Frank and Myrna are coming with us and Bill and Josephine are there already. Would it be easier to get six?"

I explained this is not the preferred large block. And I suggested that after he got here he might find another show they could all take in.

"Good idea," he said. "We were thinking of driving up there. But we decided to fly so we could spend more time with you. And we'll get out to the Fair the best way we can."

"How's that?" I asked. "By bus?"

"No."

"By taxi?"

"No."

"By subway?"

"No."

"I hate to tell you this," I said, "but our car is laid up in the garage. When were you figuring on coming here?"

"First two weeks in August."

"Well, isn't that a coincidence. We've been planning coming there the first two weeks in August and we hoped we'd be entertained by you and Helen and Ellen."

"Elaine," he said.

"Excuse me, Elaine."

"That's a bad break," he said.

"Well, that's life. Glad you called, though. Say hello to everybody."

"Yeh, same to you. And say hello to your wife, Mary."

"Jane," I said.

"Yah, and to Jane, too—how old is she now?"

"I don't know. She won't tell me."

As he was hanging up I heard him saying to his wife, "How big can you get? Can't remember old friends."

He-and-She
Talk

I<small>F</small> Y<small>OU</small> happen to be married to a nonwriter, which
unfortunately I am, and you yourself are a writer of
sorts, you get a lot of little extracurricular writing
assignments. They run from a birthday greeting or a
note of thanks for a gift received to a violent letter to
a taxi company or the mayor. In the natural course of
events her letter-writing assignments would be no
more degrading than the usual run of marital assignments—carrying out the garbage, mowing the lawn,
changing a light bulb in the ceiling at the risk of life
and limb. But, as if I didn't have enough problems in
my daily TV writing assignment, Jane used to insist
on editing my letters and re- and rewriting.

These story conferences would take place after she had assigned me, for instance, the task of writing a birthday telegram to Leon, her favorite brother.

"Make it clever," she would say.

So I'd think it over and come up with "Happy birthday, Old Man."

She wouldn't like that at all. "It makes him sound like he's an old man."

"He is," I'd volunteer.

"But you don't remind him he is on his birthday! It will depress him. It should be something gay and clever, like 'Many Happy Returns.'"

"How about sending that?" I'd ask.

"No, I mean say that but say it cleverly," she'd respond.

Jane doesn't know it but this is known in the professional writing medium as the executive producer approach. Every television writer comes up against it every week and there's nothing to do but sit down and try to come up with the idea projected—but cleverly. There is one difference. In TV the pay is a little higher than what a writer gets for writing birthday greetings to Leon.

My executive producer is a special case. For fourteen years she delivered a thousand or more malaprops over the radio and she is a victim of occupational disease. In everyday conversation she still manages a few malaprops, unthinkingly. I was not surprised recently to hear her admonish me (for trying to do too many things) with the line, "You're running around like a chicken with its hat off." And recently when she was talking about someone who got his comeuppance for a small slight she said: "Well, time wounds all heels." In this instance there was a pause and she asked: "Is that right?"

I said: "I think it's time heals all wounds."

"Time heals all wounds?" she asked. "What does that mean? That can't be right. Well, anyway. . . ."

In character on radio, she wrote letters to mother. One ended with: "P.S.: Guess who died."

I offer these as some slight nod toward justification for the assignments I now get at home. But in the past few years there has been one change—the editing and story conferences are out. She states the premise of the letter I am to write cleverly and I go to the typewriter and write it and mail it. No blue penciling, no rewrites. And it was thus when last Christmas a friend sent a case of vodka.

The letter I wrote thanked the friend for the case of medicine and related that, according to the instructions on the bottle, we are now taking it every hour. I mentioned that Jane and I had quite a discussion about how it should be taken. Jane had insisted it was meant to be taken in tomato juice. My idea was that it is best taken with a couple of onions and a twist of lemon peel. Thanks to their gift the discussion waxed into a full-blown recriminatory argument, I wrote. We finally settled on taking the medicine with nothing more than a couple of ice cubes. And in a final flight of fancy and a burst of ungracious receiving I said the drink is now known around here as "Marriage on the Rocks."

The agreement I have with my executive producer is that she not read the letters that she assigns me to write; just sign them and leave their quality of cleverness to my judgment. She signed the letter. I mailed it.

A few days later she reported she had received a peculiar note from our friends who had sent us the case of vodka. They didn't say so, but she read between the lines that they were not getting along too well— something about their marriage being on the rocks. She asked if I had sent them the thank-you note. I said I had. Then I wondered aloud: "Who'll get the custody of the note?" She laughed.

"What are you laughing at?"

"Marriage on the rocks," she laughed. "Sounds like the name of a drink. That's the kind of clever note you should have written them."

Anyone interested in buying a half-hour TV domestic situation comedy? Let me set the scene for the first episode.

The wife spends two or three of the winter months in a hotel in Florida, while the husband commutes between the winter resort and New York. During the time that he's away his wife makes friends out of strangers whom she will never see again but whom she insists on introducing to the husband when he returns. For this outline we will call the husband Everyman and the wife Jane.

Well, Everyman, when he goes away to rest, doesn't relish meeting these new and transient friends. He has come down to relax in the sun and to acquire a tan.

"I met this woman who admires you greatly," she says. "I promised I'd introduce you to her. Be friendly. Be pleasant."

Everyman rises heavily from his lounge and, dripping from every pore with suntan emollients, drags himself over to meet this woman who admires him greatly.

"This is my husband," Jane says.

"Oh?" the woman replies. "I thought he'd be shorter."

"I'm sorry," Everyman replies. "I'll try."

As they saunter away Jane accuses Everyman of being unpleasant to her friends. This leads to dialogue you would have to hear to believe. And believe me I've heard it.

That afternoon Everyman, drowsing fitfully in the sun, is shaken out of his tan when he hears his wife suddenly shout: "Well, look who's here! Did you just come down?"

As the greetings continue across space, he opens one eye and sees a young couple at a neighboring cabana.

"It's Freddie and Sunny," Jane voce sottos. "You met them here year before last."

"Oh yes," says Everyman, lying in his teeth and closing his eyes.

"Go over and say hello to Freddie and Sunny," she says. "Be pleasant."

Everyman rises, walks over to the girl, and says "Hello, Sunny."

"I'm Freddie," the girl replies. "He's Sunny."

Everyman returns wearily to his lounge, where Jane complains that he did that deliberately to embarrass her.

"You even met her mother year before last," she says.

"And what's her mother's name—Robert?" he replies.

"Your attitude," she continues, "is not conducive to making new friends. It's not even conducive to making a good marriage relationship. I try to conduce your friends; the least you can do is try to conduce mine."

This is not dialogue in the hi-camp metier. It's hirage and is documented in all accuracy. Also it says a little something about one aspect of marriage with which every husband and wife may identify. And it's for sale.

But there will not be any takers. Salable television situation comedies require something more than dialogue and a point of view. Or, as one network executive put it to me recently: "If you can come up with a situation comedy that has a gimmick, we'll buy it."

"What do you mean, gimmick?"

"Well, there's 'My Mother the Car' where the mother dies and comes back as the voice in the car. Or there's 'The Smothers Brothers' where one of the brothers comes back as an angel. Do you have an idea along those lines—with a gimmick?"

"Well, yes, I do have a gimmick," I said. "But it may seem a little too startling to you."

"Nothing's too startling for TV. What is it?"

"Well, this may be a little too unusual right now. But in my situation comedy the characters are all living."

He shook his head.

"Too far out?" I asked.

"We're looking for shows that will get a good rating," he said as we parted.

A good rating, for the uninitiated, is a rating a program gets when it has a good time spot on a network. A good time spot is a spot immediately preceding or following a program that has a good rating on a good night. A good night is what we bid television at 7:30 when we look at the high-rated Nielsen programs.

And if you're looking for a gimmick, try this one— won't it be spooky when they discover that the 1,100 people who watch television for Nielsen are the only people still watching it?

Like
Is a Many-Splendored
Thing

THERE is too much love in the world and not enough
like. Love has been so obfuscated that nothing seems
to escape the objective complement of which it is
predicate.

People love cheeseburgers. A woman's hat is loved.
A man's tie is loved. A sunset, a movie, a pair of
Bermuda shorts, an ocean voyage, a broiled lobster
are loved. Paris in the springtime is loved. Love, they
say, is where you find it. The only place you were able
to find *like* in recent days was in like the advertise-
ments of Winston cigarettes.

Love trips lightly upon the tongues of the emotional
where a little *like* would make for an endearment more

enduring. People are always falling out of *love*. No one ever falls out of *like*. Where *love* is too often demanding, *like* is most often understanding. When a girl, entwined in the arms of her boy friend, looks up at him soulfully and asks "Do you love me?" there is a quick, automatic answer: "Of course." Should she ask "Do you like me?" there is a fumble in the backfield, he makes a quick recovery, and drives through for a touchdown.

"Like you?" he replies, "I love you!" She sighs happily. She has forgotten the question. She loves the answer.

I learned early in life, before there was a Dear Abby to whom I could write for advice, the difference between these two verbs. This is a true *like* story. True but sad:

Once upon a time, many many years ago, when I was a boy in school, my arithmetic teacher drew two horizontal lines on the blackboard and proclaimed: "These are two parallel lines. No matter how far I extend them, even to infinity, they will never meet."

I sat bolt upright, halfway out of my seat. She looked over at me and asked, "Are you ill?"

I said, "Never meet?"

She replied, "Never."

I sat back, depleted, heartbroken. My every day in that classroom became a traumatic experience. She left the two parallel lines on the blackboard for weeks, and every time I saw them I saw two lines which would never meet, never fall in love. It was the saddest thing I'd ever heard.

In my mind the two lines soon became a boy and a girl destined to spend their lives side by side and never, from here to infinity, meet and fall in love. Then I began to rationalize. They don't have to fall in love. Why can't they just meet and like each other? At some time along the road from here to infinity they could walk together hand in hand or go to a movie or have a soda. I was desolate.

I must say it hadn't bothered me much when teacher had drawn a square on the blackboard and announced that four sides of a square are all the same size. I remember thinking only that it was rather square to be the same size. But I didn't go into shock. I remember when she told us that in a right-angled triangle the square root of the hypotenuse is equal to the sum of the square roots of the other two sides. I thought anybody mixed up in a triangle deserved what he got. Even the rectangle, which has two sides longer than the other two, never bothered me because they were two boys and two girls meeting on the corners and holding hands. If I seemed too preoccupied with everything materializing as boys and girls it's because I skipped the birds-and-bees stage and got right to it. I never was an outdoorsman.

Down through the years, whenever I saw two parallel lines, I got that old heavy feeling. But just the other day I read that a scientist at Mount Palomar has a new theory. The basic geometry of space is curved, he says, and two parallel lines could meet in space if extended far enough. And high time!

Where now Miss Gilliam, who was so sure they would never meet? And where now the dictionaries that so smugly defined parallel lines as "extending in the same direction at every point so as never to meet"? And where now those two innocent parallel lines she so carefully drew with a ruler on her blackboard? I know where they are—out there in space somewhere, not realizing that the basic geometry of space is curved and it is now legal for them to meet. Meet, parallel lines! Meet and hold hands and fall in like.

And like in all true like stories, live happily ever after. Period! End of piece. At least that's what I thought. But I live in that high rent district known as Fool's Paradise. If you didn't discover any error up there you are obviously not a *Saturday Review* reader. The letters poured in.

If you ever feel unloved, unwanted, uncouth, uninvited, unphoned, unwritten to, and forgettable, just write a piece for *Saturday Review* and make a mistake in grammar or arithmetic. My friends, you will be phoned and written to as if you were Dear Abby.

A few weeks ago there was a column here deploring the fact that there is too much love in the world and not enough like. It was a delicate little piece of writing, I thought, fancifully setting forth that people love crenshaw melon, a necktie, a sunset, a hamburger with onions, and in the same breath they say they love each other. *Like* has become the neglected verb. And unfortunately so, because people are constantly falling out of love. Seldom does anyone fall out of like. And so on.

In developing this sensitively romantic hyperbole I somehow got entangled with the hypotenuse of a right-angled triangle in which I wrote that at school I was taught the "square root of the hypotenuse is equal to the sum of the square roots of the other two sides." Well, what can I tell you! The minute the issue hit the stands I was hit with four telegrams. Bells rang, postmen rang, and what a wringing of hands at the desk of the editor at *Saturday Review!*

The editor reminded me that any twelve-year-old knew that the square of the hypotenuse is equal to the sum of the squares of the other two sides. And his only regret was that the magazine's policy did not permit the hiring of twelve-year-old writers. This is the same editor, Mr. Jim Fixx, who could have fixxed it—my friend, my counselor, my talking encyclopedia who phones me at two in the morning to announce he is deleting a superfluous comma after "Oh say," as in "can you see."

This geometric mistake was not easily made. As I tried to reconstruct the rule, I was torn between vaguely recalling two versions of this Pythagorean theorem. I could have chosen one or the other by cutting high card for it. But we don't operate in such a vacuum in this office. We have this computer machine into which I placed the written question: "Is it the

square root of the hypotenuse equals the sum of the
square roots of the other two sides, or is it the square
of the hypotenuse equals the sum of the squares of
the other two sides?"

The machine went to work, mulled it over, blinked
a few lights, tilted, and coughed out an answer that
read: "What was the question again, please?" So out
came the deck of cards. And that's how it happened
that I revised the theorem of Mr. Pythagoras (530 B.C.
—before computers). In defense of my machine I must
add that it is a product of the ABM people—Abacus
Business Machines—who should have stayed with
turning out abacuses—or abaci. I don't want any letters
about that. They are both preferable. Or about that.

The letters received represent a cross section of *Saturday Review* readers—a very cross section. They came
from teachers, from lawyers, from housewives, from
patients in hospitals who, having finished the Double-
Crostic, drew diagrams for me proving the theorem.
Coincidentally, they all used the figures 3 and 4 for
the sides to prove that the hypotenuse was 5, with the
figures enclosed in those little ice cream cones with the
tails. And some of them asked irrelevant questions such
as "and how would poor Mr. Euclid 'like' the adapta-
tion of his theory of parallel lines in a plane put to
elliptic or hyperbolic geometry?" I put that one into
the machine and the card came out: "Please, not while
I'm eating."

When it comes to digging out the fundamental
verities, computers are not in the same league with

Saturday Review readers, who now have sent me to the blackboard, where, before the entire class and the ectoplasmic Miss Gilliam, I pay the price of ignorance:

The square of the hypotenuse is equal to the sum of the squares of the other two sides. The square of the hypotenuse is equal to the sum of the squares of the other two sides. The square of the hypotenuse is equal to the sum of the squares of the other two sides. The square of the hypotenuse is equal to the sum of the squares of the other two sides. The square of the . . .

Somewhere
over the
Rainbow

A LETTER arrived not long ago from the RCA Service
Company of Camden, New Jersey, personal physicians
to my TV set for many years. And not a moment too
soon, because all summer my set has suffered an
agonizing siege of the reruns and now must be put
into shape to receive all these new goodies the networks have been promising us.

What's needed most for more enjoyment of my TV
set, the letter says, is a program of better-planned
maintenance. Actually, what is really needed is a maintenance of better-planned programing. But the RCA
Service Company promises only to give "complete pro-
tection to the parts and tubes of your color TV set."

It does nothing for the parts and tubes of the vice presidents in charge of what we see on TV.

In any case, I've been doing business with this nice company a long time—about ten years, if my otiose memory serves me—even before color came into our spectrums. Every season this letter came, the bill for a year's service was paid in advance, and the parade through our apartment of the service men with their little black first-aid kits was constant. Skilled of hand, quick of eye, they turned a screw here, tightened a nut there, and breathed new life into our TV set. Then came color and I must say nothing seems to help.

Oh, the men still come! Many of them think of our living room as their home away from home. The little lady plies them with colas and matches and entreats them not to lay their black tools on the white vinyl flooring. But their interest is color. They fiddle and faddle with hidden knobs and tubes until they are satisfied that the color is in order again. Little do they know that when they leave and slam the door, even ever so lightly, the knobs and tubes fall back into disrepair and the color is drained from the cheeks of our set.

And do you know how their letter refers to this phenomenon? "One of the miracles of the electronic age." Honest. I quote from their letter:

"Dear RCA Victor Color Television Owner," it begins. I've been doing business with them for many years. Wouldn't you think by now it would be simply "Dear Victor"?

To continue: "For some time now you have been enjoying one of the miracles of the electronic age—color television!"

The exclamation point is theirs.

"We trust that during that time you have enjoyed many fine months of great entertainment." Now what channel do you suppose they've been watching?

"Naturally, you'll want to make some definite provision for the future serving of your color receiver. Much more enjoyable than black-and-white TV, your color set is a prized possession."

Now hold it just one darned minute, fellows. In the first place, I think we should stop referring to them as "color" sets. These days the word has an unpleasant connotation. In my home there are two TV sets. One is black and white. The other is red and green. Those are the only two colors we can depend on with our set. No matter how many times you come to the house, no matter how long you fool with the set, by the time the "Tonight" show comes around everything is either red and green or green and red.

I take that back. There are times when the colors return unexpectedly. The other season while watching the Yankees I saw Mickey Mantle chase a fly ball across the most beautiful orange grass you ever saw.

There is one other place I get nice color on my red and green set. And that's while watching a show that is in black and white. During this show there is a lacy border of rainbow colors on the right side of my picture. I get the feeling they're waiting in the wings for a show in color to come along and they can do their stuff. Needless to say, most of them fail to show up. Red and green, of course, are always there, and sometimes mauve. But mostly just red and green—neither of which is my favorite color.

And even, sometimes, one of those colors fails me. While watching "Meet the Press" the other evening on my red and green set, I heard Lawrence Spivak and Frank McGee ask some rather pointed questions of Robert Welch of the John Birch Society. When he answered and didn't blush I knew my red was gone. On the other hand, the set probably felt Mr. Welch's antipathy.

Former President Dwight Eisenhower and William Miller, the late Republican National Chairman, are in accord on one subject—that television cameras should be barred from the floor of the Presidential conventions. If this is accomplished, they claim, it will reduce the duration of a convention to two days.

Well, yes; maybe. A better solution would be to cut off the air conditioners. Between the heat of July and August and the hot air of politics, that'll do it. Or another solution would be to keep the delegates away from the cameras. I don't remember noticing any delegate who was exactly camera-shy. As a matter of fact, every delegate I've seen who was approached on the convention floor by a TV reporter immediately assumed that look of *"Where is it? . . . over there? . . . the red light? . . . oh yes!"* Followed by an immediate shifting of profile and a huge, strained smile. Yet I fear no one will heed these solutions.

The popular sport nowadays seems to be to bar television from newsworthy happenings. Some of our judges, for instance, have barred the camera from trials of front-page names. Now it's the national conventions. But nobody has bothered to keep cameras away from the intimate affairs of the inhabitants of "Peyton Place."

The complaint by Mr. Eisenhower is that TV viewers of both conventions come away with a picture of confusion, noise, and impossible deportment. Actually, this is putting the elephant and donkey before the cart. If the confusion, noise, and impossible deportment weren't there, the cameras wouldn't be, either. Nobody yet has thought of barring the cameras from South Vietnam, where confusion, noise, and impossible deportment are rampant. Was the General suggesting that this protracted war could be cut in half by barring TV?

An
Apple
a Day

A LETTER that came from a friend complains that in
these medical symposiums I have been treating doctors
irreverently. It's an objective opinion. He just happens
to be a doctor—Dr. Milton Reder. He happens to be
the same doctor I saw at the club playing pinochle one
night. He was playing with another doctor. The bid-
ding was furious. My doctor bid 300, the other doctor
said 330, my doctor responded with 340, and the other
one with 350. My doctor studied his hand more closely
than he does an X ray, I can tell you. Finally, in disgust,
he looked across the table at the other doctor and said:
"I hope all your patients get well!"

Actually my intent is not to treat doctors irreverently. I only say, as kindly as I can, that when it comes to treating hypochondria they don't know what the hell they're talking about. I know because I went through twelve years of it and more doctors than you can shake a thermometer at, and I'm better qualified to diagnose and prescribe for hypochondria than any of them. And that includes Drs. Kildare and Casey. And you can throw in Raymond Massey.

My first meeting with a new doctor during my early hypochondriacal period was at 2 A.M. in a hotel. He arrived from his suite in the hotel disheveled and wearing a costly silk robe. He listened to my complaint—rapid heartbeat, the feeling of breathlessness—and offered me a sleeping pill. I said I don't use sleeping pills. He told me to go to sleep. Then he asked for a glass of water, swallowed the pill, and went back up to his suite.

As I indicated, I'm not a sleeping-pill man myself. Over a year I probably take six or seven. Singly, of course. Although I had at one low point thought of taking them all at once. I finally settled on slashing my wrists. That didn't work either. Those electric razors are no good for close-in work. But it did get me some attention, which, after all, is only what every first-class hypochondriac is looking for.

For instance, even now, when I'm able to feel all these mystic aches, pains, and discomfitures with some equanimity, I still walk into my doctor's office for a verbal checkup. The other day he asked me how I was feeling and I said not too well and I went on to describe my problems from head to toe. It was a brilliant organ recital, sprinkled with clinical terms—syndromes, edemas, habit-forming—all the things I've picked up from the back of patent medicine bottles. When I had finished he said, "Did you get to see the World's Fair?"

Which is not conducive to a complete recovery or even to a comfortable convalescence. So I fell back on my own cures. One of these includes listening raptly to all medical commercials on radio and television and choosing the appropriate medicines for my symptoms. These are often misleading. For instance, the headache tablet that cautions you not to shout at Billy because he left his bike in the driveway. This is so wrong! The thing to do is shout at Billy and get it off your chest. Otherwise this inner turmoil builds and you wind up with ulcers. It's only later you discover they also make something for ulcers.

And the subject of headaches recalls the time my mother came to New York on a visit—a gentle, soft-spoken, white-haired lady of eighty. She confided to me that she was being bothered by constant headaches. I examined her. My diagnosis was that what was causing the headaches was her eyes and what was indicated was a change of glasses. So I took her to one of my many doctors, a specialist in that area.

I thought he treated my diagnosis rather offhandedly because he ushered her into his private office and asked me to have a seat in the waiting room. According to the story as my mother told it later, he looked into her eyes, her nose, her ears, and came up with the announcement that all her teeth would have to come out. She took out her upper and lower plates and handed them to him.

And Now
a Brief Message
from . . .

THE OTHER evening I was watching an old movie on TV. Van Johnson was a soldier in World War II and Elizabeth Taylor was a girl he met on a pass in Paris and they fell in love and were having dinner in a bistro one night and Van got a message that he had to get back to the war for fifteen minutes and he had to leave quickly.

It was raining and he tried to find a taxi that would take Elizabeth home while he was tending the war, but there were no taxis and Elizabeth said, "You go ahead, darling. I can get a taxi myself. I'm a big girl now." So he dashed off and we saw Elizabeth start up the rainswept street. She hailed a taxi but it skittered right past her. Off duty, no doubt.

This faded to the next scene, in which Elizabeth was taking the nasal test for cold prevention and she said it had miraculously cleared her nasal passages right through the cotton in the glass tube through which she had inhaled. I looked more closely and realized it wasn't Elizabeth at all, so adroitly had the fade been made from the movie to the commercial.

Not being a habitual old-movie watcher, I haven't acquired the knack of separating the message from the movie, or the flam from the film. But I better get with it if I'm going to be a TV viewer because the networks these days are buying up old movies just as the old movie theaters in their day used to buy up popcorn. And you don't buy an old movie for peanuts. A network recently bought three old Sam Goldwyn movies for $750,000 apiece, with permission to show them for only two years, and then only twice a year. So you can readily see it takes a lot of mouth and hog wash to amortize these senescent cinamae.

A typical opening for such a movie is: The first half of this movie is brought to you by 007, the hair tonic that gives a man the license to kill, *and* Winston, the cigarette that tastes good *as* a cigarette should, *and* Carnation, the instant balanced breakfast, *and* Vicks cough cure, which now comes in lozenge drops. Well, that's OK. I'll buy all that. It's an expensive deal and the networks are not in business for their health, no matter how many cures they show us. But instead of demonstrating one of those four, they suddenly showed us a bottle of blue rinse Halo and a scene at a boys' camp where the little chap used anti-cavity Colgate.

Well, after two and a half hours the old movie you're watching begins to take on a new story concept. Subconsciously the characters begin to blend with the

players in the sponsors' vignettes until they form a
kaleidoscopic montage of story lines the producers of
the old movies had never in their wildest Hollywood
conferences contemplated.

Which brings us back to Van and Elizabeth in Paris.
When last we left them, Elizabeth was taking this nasal
test—no, that was another girl. Van had gone back to
his war and Elizabeth was trying to find a taxi in the
rain. After a deluge of commercials we find Van returning from the war and tiptoeing into a hospital room
clasping a small bouquet of flowers in his hand. I didn't
quite know the occasion and suddenly I thought,
"Good grief, she's having a baby!" But then I remembered this was an old movie and the code was pretty
strict in those days. They must have gotten married
through those commercials.

But no, Van tiptoed to Elizabeth's bedside, where
she lay, wan and pale, except for the heavy makeup
around her eyes. He stared unhappily at her. She
stared at him. Then she smiled prettily and said, "Well,
don't be so conscience-stricken. It wasn't your fault I
couldn't get a taxi in the rain and I got the flu."

"It serves you right, Elizabeth," I said to my set. "If
you had taken that nasal spray test instead of that girl
who I thought was you, you wouldn't be lying in a
hospital looking pale and wan except for the heavy
makeup around your eyes."

Well, the story moved apace with the commercials
moving at double apace. They first quarreled, I think,
when Van lit a cigar and Elizabeth wondered if Van

would offer it to a lady. To her chagrin he didn't. Recriminations followed. He taunted her blotchy skin and she reciprocated and brought up his oily hair. One shouted lovers' quarrel followed another until one day they discovered the headache tablets which turneth away wrath. By this time I got the feeling they were hurrying their performances to make way for the next batch of commercials that were becoming intertwined with their plot.

But the movie picked up as this Parisian idyl of Van and Elizabeth hotly developed into a wedding. And this was followed by the sponsors' messages in the second half. There was a slew of them. About nine months of them because when we got back Elizabeth had a baby.

I was wrong. It wasn't the nasal spray test Elizabeth should have taken. They have another one for *that!*

Hell
on Wheels

I WOULD like to say a few kind words about the taxicab
situation in New York City. In my condition it's a
tough assignment but I'll try.

According to the Unabridged, a taxicab is a
"passenger-carrying vehicle, usually a motor vehicle,
designed to seat five or seven persons, with or without
a taximeter, maintained for hire on public thorough-
fares, or at public stations or stands but not operated
on a schedule."

Noah should have quit while he was ahead. That
last line did it. The taxi drivers in New York City operate on a very tight schedule. Their appointed rounds
are not made during rain or snow or gloom of night, or

dinner hours or theater hours or to Brooklyn or on Yom Kippur. But before passing judgment or blowing a gasket let's look at it from the driver's viewpoint. We must remember they, too, are human. Or as one driver put it to me the other night after only a brief ten-minute hassle, "I'm *only* human." To what higher plane he aspires deponent sayeth not.

As a rule taxi drivers are most cooperative. Most of them will take you any place you want to go, especially if they happen to be going that way. Very few drivers happen to be going to Jackson Heights, a twenty-minute ride from Manhattan. I got into a cab and said: "Jackson Heights."

The driver said: "Oh no. I'm not going there. I'm off duty."

I said: "Your electric sign doesn't say off duty."

Flipping it on, he said, "It does now."

I said: "The sign wasn't on when I got in."

And he replied: "It's like TV. It takes time for it to warm up."

I got out. Obviously he had a point there.

A few days later, arriving by plane at Kennedy Airport, I got another driver. Or he may have been the same one. After a time they all begin to look alike. I said: "Jackson Heights, please."

And he said: "Oh, no. I want to go to Manhattan."

So I said: "I don't want to go to Manhattan. The guy from Manhattan won't take me to Jackson Heights. Then I'll be stuck in Manhattan."

And he said very quietly: "What do you want from me? You want I should be stuck in Jackson Heights?"

So you see? They have a point. I apologized and got out.

That it's difficult to get a cab during theater hours is also understandable. One driver explained it to me the other night. (I could have sworn it was the same guy.) He said, "I don't want to get caught in all that traffic." So I appealed to his civic pride. "The theater is one of New York's principal industries," I said. "People come from all over America to see our theater." And he replied: "They're the ones that cause all that traffic. Nickel tippers, too." And away he went.

So I took a crosstown bus. You think taxi drivers are— well, some other time. The bus got me as far as Forty-seventh Street and Fifth Avenue. I walked three long blocks to Broadway in the slush and snow. It was tougher getting a taxi than it was getting my ticket. But when I got there I realized the driver was right. The traffic was awful. I was glad I didn't get him mixed up in that snarl.

This taxi situation does not pertain to New York City alone. In Miami Beach I got into a cab at the Eden Roc Hotel and went to an appointment at another hotel some distance uptown. After my meeting I got into the first cab in a line at this hotel and said: "Imperial House."

He said: "Imperial House! That's only eight blocks up the beach. You could walk it."

I explained, "I'm in a hurry."

And he said, "Walk fast."

I said, "You want to take me or not?"

He said, "Well, what can you do?" And we started. I give you an exact transcript of the conversation in that eight blocks:

"I've been waiting in that line nearly an hour," he

said. "When I saw you coming out of the hotel I figured you were at least race track."

"You want to go to the races?" I asked.

He said: "Sure! I'll make a turn up at the next corner."

"You got any money?" I asked.

"No," he said.

"Neither have I. So let's go to the Imperial House. Does everybody have to go to the race track?"

"No, some people go to Palm Beach."

"You know anybody in Palm Beach?"

"No."

"Neither do I," I said. "So let's go to the Imperial House and cut out the conversation."

It's a sixty-cent ride. I gave him a dollar and told him to keep it. He didn't thank me. When a cabdriver doesn't thank me I make it a rule to leave the cab door open when I leave. Which I did. As I walked away, he leaned way out to close the door.

"————" he shouted. "————!"

Suddenly I felt at home. The same guy who was not driving me in New York had come to Miami Beach for the winter.

What Makes
Sammy Shuffle?

From a New York Times *interview with Sammy Davis
a week before his first TV hour:*

*"Is there anything distinctive about your show, com-
pared to other weekly variety programs?"*

*"Yes," replied Davis. "There's a colored fellow who's
the host and star of it."*

IT'S ALL too confusing. Forty years ago there was a
young Jewish entertainer named Al Jolson who was
trying to pass as Negro. Today there is a young Negro
entertainer named Sammy Davis who is trying to pass
as Jewish.

What genetics has to do with entertainment at this

late date eludes me. And it certainly should have
eluded Mr. Davis when you consider the many alterna-
tive answers he could have given to the question of
how his show will be different from other hour variety
programs. He could have replied that the host and star
of the show can dance rings around any other host. He
can sing with the best. He is more graceful, more en-
ergetic, and a much greater impressionist than any
other host of any other variety program.

Mr. Davis is under the delusion that he is still in the
old show-business era of the great Bert Williams. I recall the famous poker-game sketch in which Mr.
Williams called another player's bet. The player said,
"I've got a straight flush, what have you got?" And Mr.
Williams replied, "I've got two deuces and a sharp
razor."

And what has Mr. Davis got? Nothing—only talent,
show biz know-how, a rapport with any audience,
and a sharp wit. But also, he apparently has a chip on
his shoulder. He breaks no new ground. He's no Jackie
Robinson. There was the king, Cole, a host before him.
Also the queen, Lena. And Bill Cosby, co-star of "I
Spy." Color them any hue in the spectrum and their
talent prevails.

Mr. Davis seems still to be fighting to overcome. If
he is, he's shadow boxing. Actually all he had to overcome on his first program was the appearance of two
of his guests, Richard Burton and Elizabeth Taylor.
This, as I understand it, was Miss Taylor's first appearance as a guest on a variety program. Miss Taylor is an

important star in movies and has big talents. But not for the twenty-one-inch home screen. Mr. Burton, aloof and unbending, lent a stark dignity to the program, which Mr. Davis was not able to overcome as he all but groveled before such majestic grandeur.

I don't know how well acquainted you are with these two guests but I recall reading some obscure newspaper stories about their first meeting in Rome a couple of summers ago when they starred in a movie. That was also too confusing. It seems that Miss Taylor, an English girl turned Jewish, was in Rome trying to pass as Egyptian. While Mr. Burton, a Welshman, was in a toga trying to pass as Orson. And now here they were, guests on a show starring Sammy Davis, who is —well, I've lost track.

It is quite obvious that booking this famous couple on a program of song and dance, neither of which either did well, was intended to get what is known as a high rating with a high percentage of viewers. Which, according to the decimal counters, they did quite well. Actually Mr. Burton and Miss Taylor would have enhanced the rating that night even if the host had been Conway Twitty.

But in enhancing the rating, the producers failed to enhance the capabilities of Mr. Davis. I say "producers" because in a prior statement the star had announced that any mistakes made on this show would be his. And one of the mistakes was booking these two great stars if Mr. Davis was going to spend the hour genuflecting before the presence. The only spark of the real Sammy Davis showed up toward the end of the program when he was reunited briefly with his father and uncle and they performed the Chilton and Thomas airplane glide that used to close their old vaudeville act.

The *coup d'état* for this viewer was when he hung the picture of Miss Taylor and Mr. Burton on one of his memory walls and vowed that no other picture of any future guest would ever grace that wall. Amen.

Someday Mr. Davis will return as host of a variety program. I hope Mr. Davis feels equal to the task. I also hope he feels equal. And finally I hope I will be able to say of his next show, "I come not to bury Davis, but to praise him," if I may paraphrase the noblest Roman of them all, Richard Burton.

Where
the Reaction
Is

THE REACTION began to set in three weeks before
Christmas. It is during this period that the Sunday
New York *Times* has a section headed "The Neediest
Cases." In this section are pages devoted to television.
That's when I first realized I was hooked on TV. Those
network pushers had peddled me their last Julie An-
drews, Frank Sinatra, and "Charlie Brown's Christmas"
to keep me on the junk.

The reaction of other television viewers grows more
violent with each passing week. Eyes by the hundreds
of thousands are becoming unglued from their TV sets
as they become more disenchanted with the medium.
If you haven't yet joined the revolution, arise and

break your chains! You have nothing to lose but "Mona McCluskey!"

It's only a habit, watching television. But friends, you can kick this vicious habit. I offer my personal, sordid story with the prayerful hope that you, too, may become enlightened and rejoin society, Great or small.

For fourteen long years I was a cobalt addict. My television set was on from the moment I came home from work. Before I hung my hat I rushed to turn the knob and it stayed turned on the entire evening. Through dinner we never looked at the food we ate, or at each other when we spoke.

Unashamedly I confess I watched ten or twelve shows every night. The effect was an exhilaration that defies description. I floated on cloud two and four and five and seven and nine and eleven and sometimes thirteen. During these years I luxuriated in a constant state of euphoria. I gained weight—all that beer and cheese, you know—even had delusions that all was right with the world.

Then came the great awakening. It happened gradually. At first I thought it was my vision. Things began to appear in color. I looked away and then back. The color was still there. I didn't want to ask my wife for fear of frightening her. Later I discovered she didn't want to ask me for fear of frightening me. We were too far gone to realize it. Living color had come to television—the cerise grass, the lavender horses, the brown skies, the magenta bananas, and the orange faces with the red ears.

The cry for hue had come just in time. The drabness of the entertainment had begun to seep through even to my befogged mind. But strangely enough color was the catalyst that brought on my agonizing period of withdrawal. Color did not change one stilted line of the dialogue we heard or wring one twist to a predictable plot we watched. Color only pointed up their shoddy banalities.

The abandonment of TV was by easy stages. Ten shows a night became six, then four . . . excruciating torment . . . then three . . . unbearable craving . . . then two . . . clawing at walls . . . finally one . . . this would be it . . . the monkey off my back!

But it isn't easy, friends. You come home, you find yourself staring at your set, it stares back at you—the room isn't big enough for both of you. One of you has to get out. But you can't get rid of your set. Where will you put that bowl of glass grapes? Racked as I was, a Machiavellian plan obsessed me. I could beat this set at its own game. I quickly turned on Channel 3. No program. Just a light. And I sat and read a newspaper by it.

One nefarious notion leads to another. I turned to the amusement page. Movie ads were in full bloom. I made a list of the current pictures in the cinema theaters—*The Ipcress File, Dr. Zhivago, Life at the Top, The Spy Who Came in from the Cold, That Darn Cat.* Opposite this I listed the TV fare for that evening—"Gilligan's Island," "My Three Sons," "Donna Reed," and the ever-popular "Mona McCluskey." It wasn't even close. I went to a movie.

The next night I did the list of Broadway plays— *Cactus Flower, The Right Honorable Gentleman, Luv, The Odd Couple.* And the TV list: "Tammy," "Camp Runamuck," "The Smothers Brothers," "The Farmer's Daughter." The theater by a landslide. And I am proud to say that one night I went to the opera.

And so the weaning away was accomplished. But watch out for one thing. It happened that night at the opera. During a soprano's vibrato aria I heard someone humming, "Come on over to the L and M side." I looked around. It was me.

Wine,
Women,
and Song

It was a natural evolvement that psychiatrists should finally announce that parents should initiate children into the mysteries of alcoholic beverages.

Many years ago it was given into the tender care of the parents to explain to their offspring the mysteries of sex—the birds and bees—or, as it became known, the B and B theory. More recently the parent was asked to guide the child gently into the new sounds of music—the Animals and the Beatles—A and B. Now parents are told it is J and B time, completing, as some already are murmuring, the unholy trilogy of wine, women, and song, which leads the kids down the path to the Fun City of Astray, nestling on the shores of the laughing, amber waters of Lake Selfindulgence.

But I do not hold that a family that drinks together gets stoned together. I view with no alarm the graphic picture of a child learning to bend an elbow at his mother's knee. It was she who taught him to drink from the beginning. The milk of human kindness runs deep. She will steer him a straight course so that he may handle the stuff with dignity and not become the target of the slings and arrows that beset me with no mother to guide me or to distill for me in childhood the alcoholic content of a highball.

It began at age eleven. My parents had some people over and they sat around drinking highballs before dinner. My mother noticed how left out I was, sitting quietly alone in a corner. She wanted me to join in the gaiety, at least to tell my age to the man who kept asking me again and again how old I was. I had replied the first time that I was eleven. But he kept repeating the question, which I didn't feel deserved another answer. When he finally said, "Cat got your tongue?" my mother sprang into action.

She handed me a tall glass of ginger ale with a cherry atop it. In later years this became known as the Shirley Temple highball. As I sat there sipping this tall glass of ginger ale with the cherry floating in it I made my first big decision. I would save the cherry for last! I did.

I fixed myself a refill. I relaxed, even contributed to the conversation the news that that very afternoon I had won a hundred marbles and two aggies. My mother preened. Actually I was bragging a little. I hadn't won a hundred marbles. In truth I had lost fourteen. But it was an evening for only success stories. Certainly no time for losing one's marbles.

After that initiation, when other groups gathered at the house and there was drinking, I always had my Shirley Temple. One hot night I added ice. From that moment on it was Shirley Temples with ice.

I drank myself through the next five years, hooked on Shirley Temples. Until one evening at the age of sixteen I accepted an invitation along with other kids my age to a little sociable at a neighbor's home. I was offered a drink in a tall glass and sat back to enjoy it. The taste was different—bitter, I thought. And no cherry on top. I put it aside.

One of the guests noticed. "Hey," he shouted, "you're not drinking. Here, I'll fix you a fresh one." I held it and they began taunting me. Well, insecure as I was, and fearful of offending the host kid, I drank. It made me sleepy and I found myself wishing my mother was there.

Other similar parties developed. But I didn't. I soon worked out a plan to walk quietly to the bar of a party and stealthily fix myself a Shirley Temple with a cherry on top. No one questioned what I drank. I soon became, if not the life of the party, at least a member in good standing, with the reputation of being able to drink anyone under the table.

In those days you couldn't get into a saloon until you were twenty-one. At that age I was invited by a

friend into a saloon for a quick drink. You can imagine
the fracas that followed when I told the bartender I'd
have a Shirley Temple with a cherry on top.

After my friend and I were thrown out of the saloon,
I became, and still am, a secret member of Shirley
Temples Anonymous. A Shirley Temple closet drinker.
Now would you want that to happen to your kid?

Take
My Wife . . .
Please!

THERE are the evenings when a lot of wives lose their husbands to a baseball game on radio or TV. In my home it's different. My roommate is the baseball fanatic. I like baseball as well as the next woman, but I can lie there quietly enjoying the game over the edge of a book I'm trying to read—or I could if it weren't for the noisy fan in our bleacher who tenses over the set and shouts: "Come on, get a hit, Yogi, darling." And you know he hasn't been called that in years by anyone except Mrs. Berra.

Of course, Jane is not exactly a baseball fan. She's a Yankee fan. She had a box at the stadium and never missed a game. Until one day, during a World Series game with Milwaukee, a Mr. Hank Aaron lined a foul ball into our box. I wasn't able to attend that day but she had with her three men, each eight feet tall, who rose to catch the ball, accurately deflecting it under her left eye.

Seven stitches later she swore off going to the stadium. Since then she has been watching all the ball games on television. And she doesn't even sit too close to the set, in case a ball is fouled off. But her enthusiasm continues, as they say, unabated. And, I might add, unsolicited.

We are sitting at dinner after the Yankees have tried unsuccessfully all afternoon to win a game. I am discussing South Vietnam and whether or not we ought to get out of there.

"We ought to get out of Kansas City, that's where we ought to get out of," she replies. "Imagine those bums, a last-place team, beating us with a home run in the ninth, and a .219 hitter at that!"

Or I can say: "Dean Rusk says it looks like we're going to have a lot of trouble with Cambodia."

"You call that trouble? Look at the trouble Dean Chance is giving us with the Los Angeles Angels!"

Or: "I see where in Japan they're starting to holler 'Yankees Go Home.'"

"Yankees go home! We can't even get to third base."

No matter which national problem I bring up during the baseball season, she seems to correlate it to our national pastime. Whether she has something there—

whether we're playing in too many ball parks—I leave it to the experts to decide.

But it wasn't ever thus. I recall the first ball game I took her to see. Each team had scored one run in the first inning. For the next three innings they were held scoreless. I asked her if she was enjoying the game. She was. I asked her if she understood it. She did. I asked her what the score was. She said: "One thousand to one thousand." As I remember this was in the days of the lively ball.

This is the woman who today can tell you the batting averages of every player in each league and who now calls every baseball player a bum except Tom Tresh, Bobby Richardson, Roger Maris, Mickey Mantle, Elston Howard, Tony Kubek, Joe Pepitone, Clete Boyer, and even the whole pitching staff except when one is chased to the shower. And even then she leans over the set and murmurs: "Go rest, darling, you'll feel better next time out, you darling bum you."

At one time she had a box at the Polo Grounds. It wasn't that she loved the Giants but she hated the Dodgers and used the box only when the Giants played the Dodgers so she could root against them. It was the year the Giants and the Dodgers had that playoff for the National League pennant—the year Bobby Thomson made baseball history with his home run. Every game had been crucial, but this was the final and deciding game. I was away on business. I called her from Paris. No sooner had I said hello than I heard, from three thousand miles away: "We win. The bases are

loaded. Bobby steps up and hits a home run. We win!"
She was shouting hysterically in the historical present.

This from a woman who, when I took her to her second ball game, thought it horrible sportsmanship when the umpires walked out on the field at the start of a game and the fans rose and the band played "Oh say can you see?" Of course, now that she knows all the refinements of the game, she recognizes umpires for what they are. Robbers!

Scrambled
Egos

THERE are some cowards—and alphabetically I head the list—who won't get into a wrangle unless they're certain they can win it. This unfortunate catering to an egotistical fantasy, that if we can't out-logic the opposition in debate we can at least out-clever it, often finds us winding up a poor second.

There were two such recent comedic-tragic instances in the last election. I was in one and a man from Toledo, Ohio, was in the other. While they are disparate, they are relevant to my point, which is that neither I nor the man started the argument and that we both would have been better off had we been content to leave the status at quo. My excuse is that I'm sick.

In Toledo, the man, as you may have read in the dailies, is head of a corporation that owns a large office building. While he was traveling abroad and unbeknownst to him, the rental manager leased for four months, at $300 a month, first-floor office space to the Toledo Conservatives for Goldwater organization. That seems innocuous enough—except for one detail. Our Toledo man happened to be a National Democratic Committeeman.

Well, that was the dilemma our man walked into on returning from abroad. But he had two obvious choices, either of which would have hushed the whole thing up. One, he could have taken the first boat back. Two, he could have called up President Johnson and explained he was abroad when it happened. Actually, he had a third choice—a combination of the first two— taking the first boat back, then calling to explain to the President from overseas. It would have been safer. I'm sure the President would have understood; no Johnson-come-lately to big business, he.

But instead, what did our hero do? He became clever. He announced through the newspapers that the rent he received from the Goldwater-Miller organization would be turned over to the Johnson-Humphrey campaign fund. Clever thinking? The joke was on them —right? Except for one detail. One day he passed his office building and saw a huge portrait of Senator Goldwater pasted up in the window. That did it. He decided to make them move. Well, you know how easy it isn't to move a conservative from a fixed position. The wrangle was on. And the Goldwater group claimed that two rent checks, each for three hundred dollars, had been cashed by our man's corporation and had not been endorsed to the Johnson-Humphrey campaign fund. How much simpler to have taken the first boat back.

Now, the other case. Weeks later I received in the mail a letter from the Washington, D. C., headquarters of the Republican National Committee. It stated that on receipt of ten dollars I would become a sustaining member of the Republican Party. In addition to which I would be entitled to receive their biweekly bulletin. They enclosed some attractive pictures of Goldwater and Miller.

How they chose me I don't know. Evidently they are not acquainted with my record for being a sure loser. I turned down an attractive chance to invest in *Life with Father*, which holds a long-run Broadway record, and I parlayed that with a big bet that Hitler would not win the 1939 plebiscite. Anyway, I should have skipped the whole thing. But I too decided to be clever.

On the group picture of Senator Goldwater and Mr. Miller I ran an ink mark across Mr. Miller's image. Then I returned it to them, writing that I can't stand Mr. Miller since Senator Goldwater had said the reason he chose Mr. Miller as a running mate, who might some day become President, was that "he drives Johnson nuts." But I enclosed a check for five dollars and said they could send me the biweekly every other biweekly. Clever thinking, right? They would return the check. End of joke—or so I thought.

A few days later I received in the mail from their headquarters a receipt for the five dollars, attached to a card that announced I was a sustaining member of the Republican Party. The receipt was signed in their own scrawls by Mr. Miller, Bob Wilson, Courtney Burton, and a fourth one I can't quite make out—looks like Button Gwinnett. Also they enclosed a bumper sticker.

So, in spite of not paying the full assessment I am now a card-carrying member of the Republican Party. A half-assessed member.

Instant
Critic

THE THEATER, like its bastard art-form offspring TV, has been having its unbelievably ludicrous moments of travail.

In television an unfriendly network preferred showing "I Love Lucy" with Lucille Ball instead of "I Hate War" with Senator Fulbright. This brought down on the medium the wrath of the press.

In the theater the producers vented their spleen on the press when Stanley Kauffmann, New York *Times* drama critic, announced he would have more time to write a meaningful critique if he attended the final night of a play's Broadway preview rather than rush to his desk and meet his paper's late-city deadline.

Broadway producers immediately rushed into print to complain that a final preview is the crucial performance necessary to a play's polished quality. Also, though they didn't mention it, the theater has its own opening-night laugh and applause track, which includes shouts of "Huzzah," "Author," and "Go, go, go!"

I have great empathy for Mr. Kauffmann's appeal for more time to write his review and I would like to say a few words in his behalf. But I can't. I happen to know an instant critic who can review a play swiftly and with a clarity so perceptive that it never fails to astound me. I am married to her.

First let it be shown for the record that she has great contempt for the critics and their ability to control the longevity of a play's run. I quote: "It's un-American for actors on the stage to be at the mercy of twelve old men sitting as a referee."

This is a metaphor mixed with equal parts of the Supreme Court and our jury system with an anachronistic referee thrown in to compound the felony.

But however confused her flair for picturesque language, she has a great talent for quick decisions in the matter of Broadway plays. She is not an opening-nighter. She is a first Saturday matineeer, and her reviews take two forms: "Great" and "Don't go."

Actually, she can do even better than that. Before the play opens on Broadway and is ironing out the wrinkles in Philadelphia and Boston she is able to decide whether the play will be a hit here or a flop. I might go back even further than that. When the play is first announced on the drama pages and its stars are named she can assay the play's chances at a glance.

Often this is accomplished by examining the attractive or unattractive title or the name of the theater in which it will be housed. Often it is judged by its locale. Period plays will never make it. Irish plays hardly ever. Classic plays only with John Gielgud.

At any of her Saturday-matinee openings, if she is seen standing at the bar in Sardi's restaurant ten minutes after the second-act curtain has risen, the closing might as well be put up on the call board that instant. And the longer she stands there the more unpicturesque her language becomes. Actors have been known to quail and forget their lines when they look out into the audience and notice that she has not returned to her seat for the second act.

As indicated here, she is endowed with startling prescience. And you will be surprised to hear the number of plays on which she has called her shots and to learn that she is always—well, I won't say always, but she is almost always—wrong.

Parenthetically I add the interesting footnote that she also practices hypnotism. But it's only at private parties that she works her spell on friends. And while she has never actually put anyone to sleep, guests have been seen to develop great fatigue and leave soon after she has waved her hands and recited her mystic ritual.

She has a great affinity for writers of plays. She knows one Broadway playwright personally, Mr. George Axelrod, and takes credit for having launched his career with his first play, *The Seven Year Itch*. She was noncommittal when she first read he had written a play because Mr. Axelrod was working for me at the time as a writer of radio scripts. But when the play opened and was acclaimed by the critics she quickly joined in the praise of it. And she even liked it after she saw it at her first Saturday matinee.

But she really knows and appreciates good writing. She has publicly stated that I am the best writer on the scene and has often privately asked me why I don't write a play. When I replied that I am too far along in years to take up playwriting she jeered.

"Nonsense," she said, "look how old Shaw was when he wrote *My Fair Lady*."

Sex
and the
Hypochondriac . . .

ACTUALLY, the title of this piece is a cheat and a lure, and was purposely spiced up in the hope of siphoning off three or four guileless readers of the more Cyprian publications with which our bookshops abound. The title of this latest chapter on hypochondria only indicates simply that in all my years of personal research on, and affliction with, hypochondria, I have discovered that hypos are equally divided among male and female. And that's as spicy as I'm going to get.

It's not that my former affliction has left me without a keen appreciation of a pouted lip or a symmetric convex. I still retain a roving and horribly astigmatic eye for a *femme fatale*. True, when I pick up my monthly copy of *Playboy*, I now first read through the pages of sweater and slim slack ads before unfolding the center photograph. Hypo or no, one does reach the point of seldom return.

If ever a man had a case against doctors in their futile efforts to cure hypochondria, it's I. And the first witness I call to the stand is the distinguished LL.D., Mr. Noah Webster. "A state of depression and anxiety," he says, "regarding one's own state of health, with imaginary illnesses." My case is that if the illnesses were imaginary, what were those thousands of prescriptions with which my doctors plied me, which had to be filled at my neighborhood druggist's? A pretty penny that came to, I tell you, and I really ought to demand full redress. I've often thought of taking it to court, and would have, were it not for the fact that I could foresee the other lawyer having a high time discrediting the expertise of my star witness by pointing to another line in his definition, in which Mr. Webster says that "hypochondria" is derived from the Greek word, *"hypochondria."* Surely Mr. W. could have been more thorough than that.

My neighborhood druggist could, if a lawyer twisted his arm, go back in memory some twenty years to the first day I entered his shop with my first prescription, to start the bonanza I later became. The prescription was for some mild sedative capsules which the doctor had told me would be just-what-the-doctor-ordered for my condition. We had a brief, friendly discussion about my complaint, which consisted mainly

of a fast pulse and a feeling of breathlessness. I told
him the doctor had said: "Don't worry and don't be
nervous." When I'd asked how do I do that, the doctor had written this prescription. My neighborhood

druggist said these capsules should help and he added, "See you soon." That should have been the tipoff.

During the next twelve years, as I shuffled in and out of my neighborhood drugstore, I had the feeling that as the druggist read each prescription he was becoming more and more familiar with my anatomy; could call off the number of my red and white corpuscles to the penny. He knew to the dot how many spots I saw before my eyes. My aorta was an old book, my colon a tale twice told.

One day was a crisis day. A new doctor had given me four prescriptions—pills to pep me up, pills to slow me down, a tonic for appetite, and a powder for indigestion. I went to my bank, floated a loan, and shuffled into my neighborhood druggist's with the prescriptions. As he walked back to his medical center he pointed out that he had cut down on the fountain space and enlarged the prescription area. I didn't wonder. And so the years dragged on, spent mostly in my home away from home, my neighborhood drugstore.

One weekend, I came in to find my druggist not there. He had hired an assistant, who informed me my neighborhood druggist now spent his weekends fishing. He had bought a boat; I wondered if he had named it for me. I had no prescription to fill; by now I had graduated to cures seen in television commercials. I hadn't given up doctors, you understand. I still went to them for consultation, then chose my own medication. This involved describing my condition to the assistant-neighborhood-druggist, and he was most helpful—even suggested several products I hadn't seen advertised. After a few weekends, I had brought home everything from antibiotics to zinc oxide. My medicine cabinet was known around the house as General Hospital.

I promised not to get any spicier than the title of this chapter, but I find I have to drag in a little boy-girl talk here which may get somewhat basic to say nothing of messy. Because down through the years my life with the girls has been one big mess.

For instance, when it comes to making gay, light, romantic banter with the girls I'm a miserable flop. Never aggressive, hardly ever gregarious, always on the verge of fainting, I have plodded my mumbling way through those precious, first, few boy-meets-girl moments only to discover I've talked myself out of the boy-gets-girl spot, and I wind up paying $2.10 to show in the boy-loses-girl position. It's not that I really lose the girl. *I'm* invited to get lost.

As in my golf game, the drive is still in working order. The problem is my approach. For many years on first meetings I clung to "Where have you been all my life?" This not only got me nothing but I always experienced the poignant feeling she was happy and content to have been out of all my life. For a while back there my hard sell when we met was "Are there any more at home like you?" a line I remembered working so well in the Florodora Sexette. It never did for me. I imagine it works only with a group of three girls and three fellows. And sung. But in this space age what girl has time to stand around to listen to the chorus of an old Broadway melody, circa 1900?

Having discovered that my dialogue with a new-found cutie so often resulted in my winding up a one-some, I decided at one time to add action to my banter. Along with a prop handkerchief which I cleverly dropped at the foot of my intended victim I changed the opening line to "Pardon me, did you drop your kerchief?" The answer was always "No." I was never able to follow that up with anything the slightest bit Shavian or even Balzacian. But I kept at it, and as the years rolled on I changed the prop and the line to "Pardon me. Did you drop your Kleenex?"

I will say in self-defense that my delivery of the lines was in the finest tradition of our romantic leading men, in whose various images I began materializing. My first impression (ladies and gentlemen) was the suave William Powell, mustache and all. I remembered mostly how Mr. Powell always managed to get a taxi for Myrna Loy, rain or snow; and how, when they stepped out of the cab, he always had the correct bill with which to pay the cabbie, and no stopping for change.

I never got as far as even being permitted to get a cab for any of my Myrnas. I then switched to John Garfield; then to William Holden; and in rapid and frenzied succession to three Roberts—Taylor, Mitchum, and Stack. For all the good it did me with the girls it was clear that I was coming on as Sidney Green-street.

Finally I saw my error. These images to which I hoped to be transformed were all suffering from a lack of credibility because I was still wearing my William Powell mustache. My barber, who had become emotionally, and a bit irrationally, involved in my failure to communicate with the opposition sex, shaved off the mustache and gladly.

"Shaving off this mustache," he double-talked me, "will add years to your age." But I knew he meant well and I asked for further advice. He mentioned the gray in my hair.

"I have a magic bottle of some magic stuff here that works like magic. In three treatments it will magically make your hair the color it was the day you were born."

I toyed with the idea a few minutes and rejected it. I was born bald. But maybe it *was* the gray hair! The images into which I had thrown myself were too young. That's it!

The next day I was Cary Grant. With his famous swagger and that smile on my sun-lamped face I approached the first girl.

"I beg your pardon. Did you drop this kerchief and if not why didn't you?"

Well, there was some talk about accosting, and police, and it got pretty messy. Exit Cary Grant.

It was quite by accident I hit on my most attractive image—not a young man chronologically, but not an old man glandularly. Rex Harrison, naturally. I bought the cardigan sweater buttoned down the front and the Sherlock Holmes tweed hat. I was resplendent. But the girls were not respondent.

Then I remembered that in *My Fair Lady* Rex had done so well with an illiterate girl who sold flowers on the streets of London. I wandered into a midtown Manhattan hotel lobby which had a florist shop, and in attendance was a glamorous creature, beautifully accoutered to accent the gender to which she belonged. I guessed she was only in her mid-forties. That first meeting was star-sprayed. We stared at each other silently for a long moment. It was finally I who lowered my eyes. I knew I was meant for each other. Now the problem would be to pass on that feeling to her.

"I say," I said. "You are loverly. Where have you been all my life?" (I pronounced it "bean.") The effect was beyond my wildest dreams.

"Whom do you think you are—Rex Harrison?" she replied.

In that small critique she had recognized my performance as flawless. And with the first word she spoke I recognized her performance as the illiterate flower girl. It gave impetus to my characterization. So immersed was I in Rex that I ejaculated in Rex's most anguished voice of dismay: "No, no, no! Who—not whom! The verb 'are' does not take the objective 'whom.' It's 'WHO do you think you are?'"

"I know who I am," she replied. "Whom do you think YOU are?"

"No, no. WHO do you think?"

"OK. Who do you think?"

"By George, I think you've got it."

"Now," she said, "do you want to buy some flowers or don't you?"

"Yes," I replied cannily, thinking I would order a dozen or two long-stemmed roses and present them to her.

"How about a dozen or two long-stemmed roses?" I asked.

"OK," she replied. "Who shall I send 'em to?"

"Whom!" I shouted.

"Whom!" she exclaimed.

We were playing it to the hilt—what a team—Lunt and Fontanne, Tracy and Hepburn, Leigh and Olivier, Sinatra and whoever.

"Make up your mind. What are you—some kind of a nut? Who do you want the flowers to go to?"

Suddenly I was weary and depleted. The years closed in about me and I realized what my real problem had been. I was a bush leaguer swimming beyond my depth—a puck thrown for a basket—a football player caught off base. And a lot of other mixed-up metaphors looking for a simile. "Send them," I said huskily, "to Mrs. Jane Ace."

That evening I found it at home, where I should have sought it all along. As I entered there she stood—small and erect, tried and true, firm and resolute, arms folded, foot tapping. Why hadn't I noticed before? THIS was my room! I gave it one more try.

"Well," I said gayly. "Where have you been all my life?"

"What do you mean," she said, "sending me two dozen long-stemmed roses? This is no birthday, no anniversary, nothing. What have you been up to? If you think you can get away with . . ."

Film
Flam

WHEN I was a kid we used to go to the movies, only we called it the nickelodeon. Now we go to the two-dollar or two-dollar-and-a-half-odeon. And that's not the admission to only the Broadway picture palaces. The neighborhood first-run houses also charge $2 or $2.50.

The hikes in admissions all began back a few years when the first Brigitte Bardot pictures began coming over here and were shown in neighborhood movie houses first-run. Brigitte Bardot—or BB, as she was more intimately known to her movie fans—was asking quite a chunk of the profits for her revealing films—so much so that some of the neighborhood house owners were beginning to talk about throwing in the towel if

she insisted on this high percentage. But Brigitte held firmly to it, both price and towel.

Evidently BB diagnosed the id of the American film-goer a little more accurately than did the movie owners. The price was paid gladly by a long line of ticket buyers. Soon it became the standard price for the entertainment. Irving Berlin describes it in his song about show business as "all that the traffic will allow."

In my day of going to nickelodeons there arose another BB who hiked the movie admission price. This BB hiked it 100 per cent—from a nickel to a dime. That star was Broncho Billy—Broncho Billy Anderson, the Tom Mix of the Stone Age. In one fell swoop, to my chagrin, the price went from a nickel to a dime. This made quite a dent in my bankroll since I had an allowance of 10 cents for a week's entertainment.

The 10 cents was usually divided between 5 cents for the movie and 5 cents for refreshment. It didn't take a computer to tell me I was in deep trouble. A whole way of life had been destroyed by this first encounter with inflation. Insecurity had set in—a feeling I would carry through life—credit cards notwithstanding.

The refreshment consisted of an ice-cream soda, either before or after the movie. Of course this was in the days of the five-cent ice-cream soda, in the days when they didn't build an ice-cream soda like a battleship with a gob of whipped cream on the topsail and the admiral's flag embedded in the foam, with a maraschino cherry staring at you while you sip. It was just a plain ice-cream soda, some syrup, a fizz of seltzer, and a dip of ice cream.

In later moviegoing days the soda became a bag of popcorn, which also was a nickel. Popcorn became standard equipment in the movie houses to keep the movie fan's mind off the quality of early pictures. And movie-house owners of those days have confided that the worse the picture the more popcorn was consumed.

It's the old story of compulsive eating and its relation to unhappiness. For years movies and popcorn went together like Ronald Colman and Vilma Banky. I finally kicked the habit, however, when I discovered that my wife, who always became emotionally involved in the movie, was wiping the butter from her fingers on my trousers.

But one evening, alone in Chicago, and with an evening to kill, I was persuaded by the hotel doorman to go to a movie theater to see the Liston-Clay championship fight, which was being shown closed-circuit from Maine.

As I entered the crowded lobby of the large theater I was struck by a nostalgic aroma. The scent led me to a popcorn stand. My trousers were safe so I bought a bag. Well, not a bag; it was being sold in fancy cardboard buckets—the small one thirty cents; double that size, fifty cents. With an eye for bargains and since this was a fight for the championship, I foolishly bought the large bucket and made my way to my seat in the loge.

Two kernels later the fight was over. I hadn't seen it. I had missed it all while I was busy spreading my handkerchief across my trousers as a napkin. Then suddenly they showed a rerun in slow motion. The rerun in slow motion didn't take any longer than the original.

So there I was walking back to my hotel with a fifty-cent bucket of popcorn that had hardly been touched. But that's the way things went that night. The championship fighters had hardly been touched either.

It was all a kind of low comedy joke. The only consolation was that I hadn't written the show. And a man in my business needs consolation.

The lowest form of television life is the comedy writer. The script he turns in becomes a target which the star, the guests, the producer, the director, the musicians, and the stagehands shoot full of holes. Often it is these holes that finally turn up on the living-room screen.

The script that was enthusiastically received by one and all at the first reading Monday morning is suddenly by Wednesday full of old jokes that everybody has heard; they can't remember where or when. Actually, it was just day before yesterday. At this point the comedy writer, who has been lurking dejectedly around the fringe of the rehearsal hall, is invited socially into the huddle of the star and the guests and they begin to pick his brain.

The writer is soon so worn down that the brain-pickers don't have a target. Surrounded by all this high-pressure, high-priced glamour, he is now convinced that he, too, has heard the jokes before. He has forgotten it was just this past Monday. But not without putting up a small fight—like, "Well, OK, if you think so." So easily have his integrity, his dignity, his trust in the entire human race gone down the drain.

By Friday the *new* funny lines have become old and trite and the star will ad-lib some other funny lines.

"How's that line?" the star asks the writer.

"Good," says the writer. "Use that one."

To himself he says, "Why didn't I think of that?" He did. That was the line in the original script on Monday. That he can't remember it is understandable. He has spent the intervening days of rehearsal skulking in the shadows of the TV studio dreaming his favorite dream —opening a candy store specializing in jelly beans and licorice whips as a front for an opium den.

That the comedy writer is held in this low estate is evidenced quite often by the press announcements that come out of the networks when a new show is about to be launched.

"Danny Doe has just been signed to head a new comedy variety hour. Also signed are Marlo Doe as producer, Dwight Doe as director, Gary Doe as scenic designer, and Gower Doe as choreographer."

There's a bunch of competent names to conjure with. But not one mention of writers. The show goes on the air and the following day the critics hail Danny Doe as a great new star to head a new comedy variety hour. The following week Danny Doe flops. And the critics all come out and say, "Danny Doe needs better writers." As Danny himself so humorously put it during his second show: "That's the last time I'll buy a joke from Bobby Baker." And again, "I should have known that guy wasn't a writer when he came in with a set of crayons." And yet again, "This writer should go to Vietnam. They can use those bombs."

As a footnote, and for the record, let it be noted that not once during the first show when things went so well did Danny Doe say, "Let's give those writers a raise." Or at least, "All writers are invited to have dinner with me tonight—Dutch, of course."

The comedy-writing problem has become a crucial one in television. Where are the new writers coming from? Year after year old writers are dug up in spite of the flop shows they may have written. So the writing business has drifted into a sort of closed shop. The solution, of course, is for the networks to start a school for comedy writers. One such project was developed years ago by CBS and I was placed in charge of a group of six or seven young writers who wanted to make all that easy money. Each went on to become a professional writer in the medium. Two went on to become playwrights. George Axelrod wrote the long-run *Seven Year Itch* and other plays, and is now a writer for films. The other was Neil Simon, who wrote the Broadway hits, *Barefoot in the Park, The Odd Couple,* and like that.

As for the head of that class, he still dreams his dream of a candy shop with jelly beans and licorice whips. That opium den looks better every year.

The
Nielsen
Syndrome

THE networks try to rationalize the Nielsen rating
system by pointing out that it's the only system they
have—that until a better one shows up this is the one
they will use—that it has its faults but how can anybody tell whether a show is doing the job it was intended to do without a rating?

The job the show was intended to do is sell what it
advertises to as many prospective purchasers of the
sponsor's product as they could gather. Who are the
sample's 1,130 prospective purchasers? Will they buy?
What do they do? What do they think? What is their
IQ? No one in the business seems to know. Isn't it horrible to contemplate that the entire TV output on fifty-

two million home screens is in the hands of people who may have only a little knowledge of, and only a little taste for, quality?

I can only quote Alexander Pope, who never had a gadget in his set, but who said:

A little learning is a dangerous thing;
Drink deep, or taste not the Pierian spring. (A)

(A) Pierian spring, for the benefit of "Beverly Hill-billies" fans, is a kind of creek in which the Muses (B) used to go swimmin' of a Saturday afternoon.

(B) The Muses, for the Patty Duke crowd, were ancient gods of the liberal arts. They dug poetry, music, astronomy, wind instruments, and all that jazz. Like the experts who show up on the David Susskind program. (C)

(C) The David Susskind program is a television show where guests sit around and discuss subjects like integration, politics, Cosa Nostra. (D)

(D) Cosa Nostra is a highly successful and diversified corporation which deals in anything illegal from narcotics to the numbers racket. (E)

(E) The numbers racket is a legalized business in which the Nielsen deals.

Well, not being able to beat 'em, I tried to join 'em. Recently the Nielsen people announced that since the kids seem to have taken over the television sets ("OK, mom, pop, scram—I'm taking over the set. Read a book, take a walk, go to bed. This living room isn't big enough for the three of us!") the Nielsen gadgets have been taken out of some of the 1,130 sets in which they are now installed, and are being placed in homes with children in them.

Take a letter:

Dear Nielsen:

This is to apply for membership in your 1,130 club. We have no children but I have a thirteen-year-old mind, which you will note is one over the average twelve-year-old mind. Watching television by yourself can be a very, very lonely thing. I've often thought while watching how nice it would be to know that 1,129 others are watching it with me. It's a thing with me. Freud would have analyzed it as a fixation about wanting to belong. Or that misery loves company.

I would like to get to know the other members of the 1,130 club—their names, their addresses. I would write to them and they would write to me. We could exchange ideas about the quality of programs. Perhaps I could send my fellow club members reviews of the programs by the New York critics. And they could get somebody to read the reviews to them.

I hope you will look kindly on my application. Please don't be discouraged about my above-average thirteen-year-old mind. I can act pretty stupid at times. Of course not as stupid as the ratings but pretty stupid. It's just that I have this thing about wanting to belong. Oh, why do I keep saying that! I'll come clean. It all comes down to one thing—I'm power-hungry.

I want to be one of the 1,130 who decide what 190 million people watch on television. I want to have it in my power to eliminate programs, to decimate big stars with one little decimal. I want to know what it feels like to be endowed with the power to decide who shall be a star and who shall

be a has-been—to beknight or dethrone, to enshrine or de-
base—to elect or reject—to advise or consent—to sink or
swim—to put to death or let live.

Even now the power has begun to surge through me. To
slash, to rake and rend asunder! Today Joey Bishop! Tomorrow the entire Ponderosa! I'm ready, Mr. Nielsen. How
about joining your 1,130 club?

P.S. I am a select person, just right for your sample. I am
a member of the Diners' Club in good standing.

I got no reply. Obviously I was blackballed.

But is it possible for network executives to be a little
more patient and tolerant with the new programs? Do
one or two low Nielsen ratings early in the season
justify a program's demise? Is a show with intrinsic
merit to be consigned to the junk heap simply because
1,130 anonymous Nielsen viewers point thumbs down?
Is this the ultimate and final yardstick? I hope not.

Perhaps this story will support my hopes. It appeared in the New Haven *Journal-Courier* under an AP
credit and somehow did not run in any New York newspaper. The date is August 9, 1965. This is not one of
those vague stories mentioned earlier. It has names,
places, and direct quotes.

In Bridgeport, Connecticut, lives a young man
named Edward Lemoine, age thirty-one. He was con-
tacted by telephone by the A. C. Nielsen Company.

"They asked me," he said, "if I had a television set. I
said yes I have. They asked me if it was a color set. I
said no."

He was asked if he would fill out some forms for the

A. C. Nielsen Company indicating which programs he tuned in on his television set. He agreed and they sent him the forms. He did this for Nielsen in February and July of this year and it was a nonpaying job.

Mr. Lemoine's preferences ran to news programs and documentaries. "I don't enjoy these situation comedies," he said.

They had asked if he had a television set and they asked if it was in color. One question they didn't ask. And he didn't volunteer the information that his television set had no picture tube.

Because, you see, Mr. Lemoine, from the age of seven, has been blind.

In the interview in the *Journal-Courier* Mr. Lemoine was asked what he thought of being asked to be a judge of television programs.

And Mr. Lemoine, bless him, replied: "I thought it was rather funny."

The only hope is that network vice presidents will share Mr. Lemoine's sense of fun. "None so blind as those that will not see."

Sick
Comedy

FUNNY stories about doctors are rife. One of the rifest is the one about the doctor who numbered among his patients a plumber who was forever getting sick after midnight. Doctors prefer patients who are stricken at some more reasonable hour, a preference the plumber had come to know too well.

The plumber, who was sound asleep one midnight, got a call from his doctor. There were sounds of crisis and tragedy on the other end.

"My toilet is overflowing," shouted the doctor.

The plumber sleepily replied: "Drop in two aspirin and go to bed."

But George Burns has a true doctor story to tell, not

so much a joke, perhaps, as a sick experience. Some years ago he found himself nervously, constantly clearing his throat. Day and night, without surcease, George was humph-hmphhh-ing. Friends began asking about this disturbing cacophony of throat sounds which accompanied George's every spoken word like a laugh track on one of his TV comedies. He went to all the prominent Beverly Hills specialists but they were unable not only to diagnose his complaint but to offer any advice. Finally he was told about a man in Los Angeles, a refugee European doctor, who had migrated to Los Angeles during the war and who, in spite of his small office and scant reputation, was an able throat man. George went to him.

The morose little man sat George in his examination chair and asked what the trouble was.

"I keep clearing my throat," said George. "I keep going hmphhh day and night."

The doctor asked George to open his mouth and with his head mirror peered carefully into George's throat for about five minutes. Finally he told George to close his mouth.

"Now vas is your trouble again?" asked the doctor.

"I keep clearing my throat. I keep going hmphhhh," said George.

"Vy do you do dat?" the doctor asked.

"Why do I do it?" George said.

"Don't do it," said the doctor. "That ain't nice."

"I know it ain't nice!" George shouted.

"I got no time for these kind cases," said the doctor.

"Go to your specialists in Beverly Hills. In the meantime, here," the doctor said. "Suck on this. That'll be five dollars."

He handed George a piece of hard candy.

"This is your advice? That's all there is to it?"

"No, one other thing," the doctor replied. "Before you put the candy in your mouth, take off the cellophane paper."

George was cured.

Dr. Milton Reder of Manhattan is an eye, ear, and nose man of great repute. I often refer to him as my eye, ear, nose, and stomach man, because the medication he gives me upsets my digestion. Dr. Reder enlisted in the war when the call for doctors came. He had been studying plastic surgery and he will relate the plastic operations he performed during the war at the drop of a question. If you're ever in his office, don't drop it. After a couple of years, he returned to civilian life and was welcomed back by all his patients, one of whom was a lady from the Bronx.

She was a Dr. Reder fan. Before penicillin had become popular the good doctor had performed a mastoid operation on her small son and saved his life. The woman was eternally grateful. And now she had a chance to demonstrate her gratitude. She promised she would send him many patients with eye, ear, nose, and throat problems.

"I now do plastic surgery too," said the doctor.

She was delighted.

"Oh, for plastic surgery I can send you many many

patients," she declared. "Tell me, doctor, have you got pictures before and after your operations?"

The doctor was glad she asked. He showed her dozens of noses and chins and wrinkles before and after he had performed his miracle craft.

"Oh, they're beautiful, doctor," she crowed. "Simply magnificent. Even the befores are beautiful," she added.

Of course, stories about psychiatrists abound. But a favorite, and one seldom told (stop me if you've heard it) is the one about a wealthy man in his fifties who finally consented to abide by his wife's continual suggestions that he see a psychiatrist.

On his first visit he lay on the couch and stared at the ceiling. He said not a word. The doctor waited patiently but nothing was forthcoming.

"Your hour is up," the doctor said finally. "Come back tomorrow at the same time."

The man arose, walked out, the receptionist said, "That will be twenty-five dollars." He paid it and departed.

The next day it was the same thing. He spoke not a word, the doctor sat silently waiting, nothing happened. He arose, paid another twenty-five dollars and walked out. This went on for six weeks. On Monday of the seventh week the man appeared again, sat silently for half an hour and finally spoke.

"Doctor," he said, "do you mind if I ask you a question?"

"Not at all," said the delighted doctor. "Now you're

talking. The therapy to be complete must be voluntary. Anything you want to know you may ask. What is the question?"

"Tell me, doctor," the man replied. "Do you want to take in a partner?"

But all jokes and funny stories about doctors aside, I have found most of the doctors to whom I have trudged with my hypochondriacal complaints to be competent and dedicated men. Most of them have their own private comments to make about their chosen profession. One surgeon, for instance, whom I complimented recently on an operation he had performed on a friend of mine, said: "If I'm such a good doctor why don't I have my own television show?"

Kildare. There's an unfortunate name, even for a television doctor. Actually television has never turned out doctors like we used to have on radio. My age group will recall Jean Hersholt as Dr. Christian. When Dr. Christian asked a patient to open wide his mouth, it was so the patient could say "Ahhhh," not why he hated his mother or his father.

Dr. Christian—there's a name for a physician for you. A surgeon with God as his anesthetist.

What
Are We—
Statues?

RUSSIAN scientists astonished our world by announcing they had picked up extraterrestrial radio signals sent by an exbiological object. The waves have been repeated regularly every hundred days. These regularly repeated signals will undoubtedly turn out to be reruns of "Make Room for Daddy." However, one regularly repeated signal every 180 days is the sound of pigeons returning to the Isle of Manhattan. The pigeon season officially opened this month when several thousand flew back to their own personal Capistrano, which is the terrace of our apartment overlooking Park Avenue.

These feathered tourists know that New York is a good place to visit, but they wouldn't want to live here.

So every six months they check in at our place, bag and garbage, and they visit for six months—no side

trips to the Fair, the Mets, or the Empire State Building. They stay close to home, night and day, and they're here on the American plan, except that we don't feed them. Not voluntarily, anyway.

May 1 is their day of arrival. The accommodations are long and spacious, our terrace running the width of our hotel, about half a block, with an awning and a sprinkling system as their private air conditioning to fend off the setting sun on hot summer days.

Not being pigeon fanciers, we have attempted over the years to discourage their annual visits. When they first arrived about five seasons ago, my wife, the perfect hostess she is, tried getting rid of them by standing out on the terrace and saying "Shoo!" Apparently in pigeon English this translates as "Welcome home." That same day it brought in another group in perfect formation.

That year I was appointed house detective to throw out the uninvited guests. I searched around town but it was a hopeless task until one day I came across a bonanza—a pasty, gelatin-like substance called Pigeon Repellent. And where do you think I found it? In a pet shop.

Early one morning while the pigeons slept, I smeared the Pigeon Repellent stuff along the entire terrace. Our pigeons loved the stuff. They enjoyed it as much as they did the lunches we used to eat out there during the summer months. That was the year when some gossipy carrier pigeon spread the word that we not only had an excellent and varied main course, but that we had a gelatin dessert better than cherries jubilee flambé.

The following year I read somewhere that small, multicolored whirling pinwheels would frighten them away. I decorated the terrace with small, multicolored pinwheels and the breeze set them to whirling. Not only were the pigeons not frightened away, but our terrace became their Coney Island. Now they had fun with their meals.

It was then that we decided to eliminate outdoor eating. The terrace would be used only for sun-bathing. At first this discouraged our pigeons; they were not only discouraged but also a little disappointed. Until they discovered suntan oil drippings. Although more ambrosial than the Repellent, suntan oil drippings, I discovered, are not as filling, because an hour later they were hungry again.

It's not that the pigeons are unappreciative. On the contrary, every day after eating us out of house and terrace they settle themselves comfortably on window ledges and alcoves and start thanking us, setting up a cooing that can be heard down on the avenue twenty-five floors below.

This week our pigeons have checked in again with their voracious appetites and their credit cards. They spent the first day casing the place for possible property improvements, testing the window ledges and split-level alcoves for bedroom suites, and setting up a din complaining about the excessively slow room service.

But I've saved my master plan for this season. I'm putting up a sign that says "No Pigeons Allowed." If that doesn't work I'm a dead pigeon, sure as shooting. Oops, now there's a Freudian thing if there ever was one.

Smoke
Gets in Your
Ears

DESPITE certain remarks which have gone before, I happen to love television commercials. But only commercials dealing with health. And sometimes life insurance. One of my favorites, which comes on usually as we're having dinner, is the denture plates commercial, where they demonstrate with a pencil that some gooey pastes don't hold dentures in place. (See the goo loosen from the pencil?) But the other goo sticks to the dentures. (See the pencil firmly imbedded in the goo?) This is a helpful commercial if you are a pencil.

It is, to be sure, the direct, hard sell. You know what the goo they sell will do. If you don't, you're lying in your teeth. But it's the subliminal advertising that makes me nervous. For instance, the question they ask: "Should a gentleman offer a lady a cigar?" They don't commit themselves, but they hope that a lady sitting innocently at her TV set, giving herself a pedicure, may wonder, "Why not?" No hard sell—"Get up, lady, go to your cigar counter and buy one now." The thought seeps through instead. She merely inhales the message.

There are other little one-minute novelettes equally as attractive. Consider these two little story lines, one for a cigar, the other for a cigarette. First, a boss is out of cigarettes, his employee gives him one, the boss takes a puff and gives the employee a raise. Second, a man hasn't the courage to ask for a raise. He smokes a cigar and gets the raise. If either of those two plots had seeped into an advertising agency's half-hour situation comedy show Madison Avenue would have been clouded over with a thick layer of gray flannel lint.

But I didn't make these up. I give you actual dialogue or a slightly unreasonable facsimile:

The scene is a bank. The president is out of cigarettes.

"Grigsby!" he shouts. "Got a cigarette?"

"Yes sir," responds Grigsby, "a charcoal filter."

"Ahh," says the president, "I don't like the taste of them."

A voice over says: "What the president didn't know is that Philip Morris has the coconut charcoal."

"You'll like it," says Grigsby.

The president lights it. While he lights it we see a

surgical operation being performed on Philip Morris, and out drops the brain of some advertising genius in the form of tiny granules of charcoal—excuse me— coconut charcoal, looking something like the residue of what you scrape out of an old favorite pipe.

"I like it," says the president. "Grigsby, you're due for a promotion."

The other commercial concerns the White Owl cigar known as the Invincible. Our announcer's voice says:

"The White Owl may not make you invincible but it makes you feel that way."

We see a young man nervously pacing in front of the door leading to the boss's office. He has been promised a raise and hasn't got it yet. He goes to the door— falters—steps back, tries again but can't make it. In his nervousness he lights up a White Owl cigar. He takes a puff or two, the metamorphosis takes place, and he strides in, trailing behind him a feathery cloud of White Owl smoke. The boss is off-camera but we see the young invincible man shake his cigar furiously toward the camera.

"Now see here," he shouts at the top of his invincible voice, "about my raise—I demand to know why it hasn't gone through yet. . . . Oh, it has? Gee, thanks Dad."

No charcoal granules—excuse me—no coconut charcoal granules here. Just plain in-the-raw invincibility, with a heaping sprinkling of granules of nepotism. This is a case of "who's up front that counts."

It is also obvious that Dad is not a smoker of White Owl cigars. If he had been he would have had the invincibility to throw that young weed out right on his ear.

I must say that none of these smoking commercials has ever moved me to accept its premise or its product. But I confess there is one smoking commercial that has always intrigued me. I've always had the feeling that I'd like to come up and smoke a Muriel with Edie sometime. No plot—except the one I conjure up in my weak, subliminal mind.

Personal,
But Not
Too

THE two newspaper features widely read in our home are the weather and horoscope columns. Not by me. My wife reads them to me every morning as I leave for the office. I've managed to live with her daily recitals only because of the attendant dialogue, which I will give you a sample of herewith.

"Thundershowers," she says.

"So?" I say, gazing out through a sun-spattered window.

"So, take a raincoat."

I reach into the closet and drag out a raincoat.

"Not that one. I just had it cleaned and pressed. Wear the one I got you for Father's Day."

She did. In 1961. A tissue-paper-thin, shapeless gabardine that even Shylock would not have spat upon. Much less a thundershower.

That night I return carrying the raincoat over my arm.

"What happened to the thundershowers?"

"The wind veered," she says.

"Veered?"

"The wind veered. They announced it on the radio a few minutes after you left. They hadn't expected it to veer but it veered." Veered is the word for the day.

With the horoscope column it becomes a little more complicated. Every morning, after Jane reads my horoscope to me, she also reads me her horoscope for the day. Our horoscopes are seldom compatible and this is a source of great worry to her. She feels certain our marital status is in jeopardy. She has felt this way for about thirty-five years.

It seems I'm a Capricorn. And from the way she has our compatibility figured out she must be a Montague. And you know how they got along. Any day now I expect her to suggest the hemlock bit. One day I suggested that I had never hidden my birth date from her. It was, in fact, her first question after we had been introduced.

"I know," she said, "but I thought in time I could overcome it. Being a Libra I'm well balanced."

Actually she's neither. But I don't fight that kind of talk. Being a Capricorn, I never let it get my goat. Instead I try reason, logic, and other unfair tactics, as I

do in all our misunderstandings. Most of the time I quietly quote Julius Caesar:

"Men at some time are masters of their fates," I say softly. "The fault, dear Brutus, is not in our stars, but in ourselves, that we are underlings."

"Oh yeh? And you know what happened to Julius Caesar. Shot down like a dog." Sometimes in the heat of the discussion she corrects herself and says Sid Caesar.

For several weeks at a stretch my horoscope seemed to say the same thing: "Don't sign anything today." This warning was repeated to me every morning as I left for the office. All that got me were some second notices on bills for which I had not sent checks.

For some years now Jane has developed a correlation between her horoscope and Chinese fortune cookies—the thirteenth symbol in her zodiac—the sign of the Subgum. Any night she may be found in one of these dens carefully selecting a lucky fortune cookie after a close and lengthy inspection, when anyone knows you can't tell one Chinese cookie from another. There is often a contradiction between the prediction of the horoscope and the cookie. At such times she chooses the more pleasant.

But it's when plans are being formulated for traveling South on a winter's vacation that the horoscope gets its biggest play. Certain days are advantageous to think about traveling, certain days to pack for traveling, and finally one certain day actually to travel. For this last step of the trip she adds to the horoscope *The Old Farmer's Almanac*.

Since plane reservations cannot be made horoscopically—and don't think she hasn't phoned to try—she must deduce at least a week in advance a certain propitious trend in her horoscope, which she measures up against the *Farmer's Almanac* for clear flying weather. Somehow she finally manages to match them —you give a little, you take a little—and off we go to the airport.

Once on the plane and we have fastened our seat belts, she is relaxed and content in the indisputable knowledge that her star will see her through. And once the door is banged shut and the engines begin their terrifying din, I notice she supplements it all with a softly murmured prayer. And why not? He did put the stars there, didn't He?

The
Home of the
Freeway

EVERY summer well-meaning friends with beach homes on Long Island ask: "Where are you going this weekend?" I always answer: "On the terrace." Their empathy oozes from every pore and their solicitous invitations to help get me out of the city for the weekend are so overwhelming that I begin to feel I'm the kid in the ad beseeching to be sent to camp.

There are two reasons I spend summer weekends in the city. The first is a secret reason which I never confide to anyone. I don't want to be too far away from my doctors. The other reason, and less important, is that these people who invite us haven't discovered New York City during summer weekends of July and

August. Shops closed, streets empty, it's a veritable Dodge City. All taxis are not only on duty but they climb sidewalks and kneel low on their bumpers imploring to be taken. The same sun that shines on the beaches shines on the terrace. And when it gets too hot there's the cool breeze in the shade of an air conditioner inside the apartment. And the stillness! You don't know what communing with nature is until you've sat in the golden hush of a sunny New York summer afternoon weekend broken only by the occasional hum of a defrosting refrigerator. I've always thought the mayor or somebody should turn down the sound of the waves on the beaches. It even drowns out the commercials on my transistor radio.

So we politely regret invitations to spend Fridays through Sundays. No one invites you to spend Mondays through Fridays, certainly a more desirable time to get away from the hustle and fumes and torn-up streets. It's surprising they don't. Most New Yorkers can't abide New York during weekdays. The only people who really dig it are from Con Edison.

There was a time some years ago when we accepted weekend invitations to the beaches. But they were disastrous. It was the telephoned instructions how to get there which started things off badly. The first instruction: "If you want to avoid all that weekend traffic you better start early. The best hour is late Thursday night or early Friday morning." Since this choice of hours turns out to be one and the same, 2 A.M., we decide to leave at our convenience on Friday toward noon.

Now the dictated instructions:

"Turn off at Exit 36 till you come to a Bohack. (When it was too late we realized we should have spent the weekend at that supermarket.) Turn right at Bohack till the yellow filling station and turn left at the third stop light. Our house is a half mile south of that."

By this time you don't know your south from your north so you drive back to Bohack and ask if they handle compasses. They don't. But there's a phone at the garage a half mile west. By this time you don't know your west from your east, so you drive aimlessly around and finally locate the garage. Your hosts are always surprised to hear you're in a garage.

"How did you get *there?*"

It wasn't easy. They command us to stay there and they will meet us in their car and we can follow them in. Our safari finally arrives at their split-level oasis. We are greeted by the clamor of their three small sons as if we were McDivitt and White. And the quiet week-end at the beach begins.

During our last four successive visits to the Long Island beach it rained continuously. (This was when water flowed like water.) Well, our hosts decided the night would be great for sleeping. Do you rhapsodize at, or are you an aficionado of, or have you tried to sleep to, the crackling croaking of a cricket in your bedroom throughout the entire night?

By the following morning and all through Sunday each member of the cast of happy beach-home owners had been transformed into a Jeanne Eagels. As had the small sons-of-beach-owners.

Our last leavetaking of Long Island was something less than gay. The host had offered to lead us to the main highway but as his sons came out to wave a fond good-by the tiniest of the tots fell the full length of his twenty-eight inches on the wet grass and set up a terrifying wail. We left the father administering to the kid who was now in the last stages of a scratched knee. We insisted we could find our way back to New York from Long Island without his help.

Much later that night we spent our first peaceful weekend evening in a motel just outside West Philadelphia.

Inventory

THE book could have been much longer but I'm pressed for time. This is our inventory season. At certain times of the year I take inventory of my pillbox, substituting new miracle drugs for old miracle drugs, especially those which have lost their miracle, and blowing out the dust of some of the capsules which have lost some of their dust. These are the pills which doctors have guaranteed "work like a charm." Few work like medicine.

It's amazing the number of pills which can be crowded into a watch-pocket-size pillbox, along with helpful first-aid memoranda. This includes the phone numbers, private and professional, of doctors scattered

around the city. Their accessibility is of crucial import to a hypochondriac every time he realizes he's dying.

Nothing furthers the anxiety of a hypo more than when he phones his doctor and is told by a dispassionate service-girl, that she may be hearing from the doctor "any day now." In one fit of despair I once whispered to such a nurse: "OK, when you hear from him, tell him the services will be Friday. No flowers."

So my pillbox carries the schedules of all the doctors who are thoroughly acquainted with each of my maladies. The schedules contain their office hours, their vacation periods, their bridge nights, their nights for movie- or theatergoing, their exact hours at hospitals, and, in one case, the name of a young doctor who has contracted to call me every hour since he always refuses to give me a number where I can reach him nights.

These schedules are the foundation of my pillbox, folded neatly under the pills. On opening the pillbox you are struck by a magnificent display of potions of breathtaking brilliance and in living color. I hope. I know each of them personally, recognizing them by their color, their size, their efficacy, and their side reactions.

There are pills to ease pain in tender spots, and pills to bring on pain in numb spots. There are small-cab pills which I take when riding in small taxis. There are crowded-night-club pills which I take when I go to a crowded night club. There is the hullabaloo pill which I take when I watch a certain television show; the RIP pill when a funeral passes me on the street; the middle-of-the-aisle pill to be taken in theaters when I realize the number of people I will have to discommode in the middle of an act when I feel a sinking spell coming on. (This pill can be done away with if you are lucky enough to get an aisle seat.)

The array is replete with cures to handle any contingency. Their technical names have long been for-

gotten. And over them is laid a tiny typed note in case
of sudden collapse on a street. It reads: "Don't crowd.
Give me room." Also an accordion-folded tongue de-
pressor, and a miniature thermometer which only
registers up to 68.4 degrees Fahrenheit.

To the uninitiated this may seem extreme. That is
because they are not familiar with the endless machi-
nations of an overwrought hypochondriacal mind.
When I wrote many of these sick pieces for the *Saturday Review* there was a small avalanche of mail
from fellow sufferers, to say nothing of some unquot-
able letters from several doctors. Most of the mail was
written by nervous, intense sufferers who are fiercely
fighting the bitter fight of survival. But one letter from
a lady was so beautifully phrased and tenderly offered
that one could feel the composure and serenity which
enveloped her. Why? Because she had accepted hypochondria as a way of life. And so, with the kind per-
mission of Laura W. Douglas of Terrace Park, Ohio,
I want to share it with you. She writes:

Dear Mr. Ace:

I want to thank you for the Art of Hypochondria series.
It is comforting to become acquainted with another dedicated hypochondriac, even if it is only in print, for I too
have cultivated the art and feel qualified to be classed as an
Old Master.

I was probably not more than four years old, when,
standing tip-toe on the Morris chair, I could study my
flushed face in grandpa's shaving mirror. After playing all
day and evening in 90° weather I went to bed each night

with scarlet fever. Fifty-odd years ago scarlet fever was a dread disease from which few children recovered. If a child did, baldness, deafness, blindness and any number of unmentionable disabilities were the price of survival and death was preferable. My own funerals I attended were poignant affairs. There I lay in a small casket, swathed in a white, dotted-swiss dress with lace on the collar, clutching a spray of Dorothy Perkins roses in my lifeless hands while the mourners stood their distance, unable to plant one last kiss on my cold, still scarlet forehead because they would catch *it*. The morticians' susceptibility to *it* didn't occur to me because the dead were in caskets and how they got there was none of my affair.

After coasting in zero weather I pulled my sled the weary, freezing way home from the pasture disintegrating with leprosy. No feeling in fingers, toes, ears, nose. These appendages, of course, would eventually fall off and my life in the leprosarium was a tragic, digitless, earless, noseless existence until my head fell off, at which time my sordid remains were hermetically sealed in a cast iron box and buried at sea.

As I listened to the doleful sagas of ancient great-aunts I progressed from childhood fever and leprosy to teen-age lockjaw, black plague and Rocky Mountain spotted fever. From those years on, the list of diseases with which I have been wracked is formidable, each of them caught from medical articles in the Reader's Digest and doctors' columns in the daily paper, none of them ever properly diagnosed except by me.

Strangely, I have never had a heart attack and sometimes wonder if my mechanism works with an odd assortment of pumps and pipes and bolts contrived by God in a facetious moment when He anticipated Rube Goldberg cartoons and the plastic industry. This is quite likely because recently I fell down the stairs, when turning right instead of left in the middle of the night. As I bumped and bounced there were no heart palpitations and none as I came to rest in the hall below. Nor was anything broken. The only painful results were strawberry burns from the stair carpet and some gargantuan surrealist blue-green-purple bruises.

This step into ebony space should prove that my skin and bones and plastic Rube Goldberg machinery are indestructible but only yesterday I overheard two women at the check-out discussing ubiquitous anthetritis; at least that's what it sounded like over the whirr of the cash register. Ubiquitous is defined in WNI. Anthretitis is not but I have it. If you are interested I will be happy to send you a description of the symptoms so you can have it too.

Sincerely and feverishly yours,
(Signed) LAURA W. DOUGLAS

Maybe she should have written this book.

Goldilocks
and the Three
Bears

You may have the idea that because for years now I
have glutted myself on a menu consisting mainly of
pills du jour that I have grown dull of wit, dim of
wick, and drab of woof. Not so!

Take the matter of finance, for instance. It runs in
the family. Many years ago Jane made an astute in-
vestment in government. What she did was, she bought
thousands of two-cent stamps. And when you consider
what it costs to send a letter today you may realize
the affluent position of her portfolio.

This one-upmanship has been a cross I've had to
bear for some time. So one day I decided to invade
the big street myself. I don't exactly consider myself

the wolf of Wall Street. But with some shrewd invest-
ments I recently made I have attained the status of at
least a coyote. Since the day I phoned Mr. Goldilocks
the chicken coops of Wall Street have become my
hunting grounds.

Mr. Goldilocks is a customers' man in a brokerage
office. For the past three years I've been phoning Mr.
Goldilocks, pleading with him to put me in the market,
preferably on the Big Board, which I've read so much
about, or the American Exchange or over the counter
or under the table or any way, so I can get in on some
of that big money my friends are making.

But Mr. Goldilocks always explains that he and his
three associates are bears. For the past three years
they've been feeding me that porridge that the market
is shaky and the trend is that the market is heading for
a crash. This imminent crash has made several of my
friends so rich they've raised the stakes of our bridge
games to a nickel a point, and one of them has to carry
me for the extra four and a half cents.

My embarrassingly nouveau-poor status finally
forced me to tell Mr. Goldilocks off. He's been calling
me at the office every morning after the first hour's
transactions to tell me the market is off a point at the
opening and it looks like the break is coming. He calls
me every day after the market closes to tell me the
market is up three points but not to let that fool me.

"The suckers are buying," he says.

"But Sam," I say—that's his name, Sam Goldilocks—

"Sam, my friends are all making fortunes. Let me be a sucker, too."

"Not yet," says Mr. Goldilocks. "I'll tell you when."

But at the end of one day he called—I'll never forget the day—it was the day he told me the Dow Jones averages had gone up 8.34 points. It was Rosh Hashana, the beginning of the New Market. That was the day I figured that one of my friends had made $5,726, which weirdly coincided with the date of the new year. I was furious.

"Mr. Goldilocks," I said, "Sam, I've been panting to get into the market, and now, Sam, you've made the pant too long. I want to buy."

"Buy what?" he said.

"I'll figure it out and I'll call you tomorrow."

That night I read the market page thoroughly. Tucked away in a small paragraph I found the secret key to the stocks to buy: "Since the federal government announced its stepped-up military program in Vietnam, many analysts feel the war effort has put off an economic slowdown, thus a market decline, for six months."

That was the tip I was looking for. An escalating war means an escalating market. I realized I've been mistakenly reading newspapers only for information. The papers are rich with information. Well, to hell with information. I'm going to concentrate on rich. I also realized that I'm too late to get in on all that Vietnam war gravy, thanks to Mr. Goldilocks and his bears. Now

I'll read between the lines of newspaper stories and make my own analyses.

Why, the newspaper is a veritable gold mine! It's a cinch. Nickel bridge here I come! What nuggets I panned in the murky waters of the mainstream of our America's progressive and advanced civilization. I was on the phone with Mr. Goldilocks first thing next morning:

"I want to buy twenty-five shares of Walter Kidde Company. It's on the American Exchange."

"Walter Kidde Company! I know where it is. I told you this is no time to buy any stocks now."

"Sam, I want to buy it. Didn't you read in the paper about that travesty of a trial down in Alabama of the man who is on trial for killing the Episcopal ministerial student?"

"So what's Walter Kidde got to do with that? They make aircraft accessories."

"That's your trouble, Sam. You don't read deep enough. They also make fire extinguishers. Do you realize how that's going to escalate cross-burning down there? Just think of the demand for fire extinguishers! And, oh yes, buy me fifty shares of AT & T."

"Well, now you're talking—you want telephone?"

"No, AT & T, the Alabama Textile and Towel Company. They make bedsheets. The towels are just a front. This trial is going to escalate Klan membership by the thousands."

"Look, I never heard of that company. Besides, why do you want to get into the market at this level?"

"Nickel bridge, that's why!"

"What did you say?"

"Look, Mr. Goldilocks, all I want to do is what every-body else is doing—trying to keep up with the Dow Joneses."

How
to Not Write
a Book

THIS is a sloppy way to do business, especially for a renowned publishing company like Doubleday. It was last November they called to ask me to write a book and could I have it ready by next March. Well, last November March seemed an eternity away so I said sure.

How a successful outfit like Doubleday ever gets any book published is beyond me. Not once from November to March did anybody call to ask how the book was coming along. Which it wasn't. Nor did they ask if I had started it. Which I hadn't. They seem to have assumed that my word was good. Which it isn't. They must have some people up there at Doubleday who could have kept at me. Their stationery says "and Company."

That a book ever hits the stands must be sheer luck. It is unthinkable that Hoe ever visualized his printing press would be a partner to such sleazy maneuvering in the book business. And it seems typical of all publishing houses. Let's take the great firm Simon & Schuster. But let's go back twelve years to see just how nonchalant a publisher can be about getting a book written.

It was in 1953 that a gentleman called from S & S to invite me to lunch. He asked if I had ever given consideration to writing a book. I replied I had, hadn't everybody? He asked if I would write one for his firm. I said sure.

The next day I received a check from S & S for fifteen hundred dollars. I called the man and asked about it. He said it was an advance. I tried to explain I wasn't sure when I'd write it, or if. He was sure I would. A year later he called to inquire. I explained I hadn't started it and did he want his check returned. He was deeply hurt. He explained the check was "thinking money." So all that day and the rest of another year I thought about "thinking money."

It was during that second year that I had a call from Doubleday. That man asked me to lunch and wondered if I would write a book for his firm. I said I might. He didn't ask nor did I volunteer the information that I was already in the process of not writing a book for Simon & Schuster. The next day I received a check from Doubleday for two thousand dollars.

I thought briefly of returning the check but I recalled how sensitive they were about their "thinking money." Then I began visualizing that if I got "thinking money" from all the publishers I could retire without ever having written a word.

But that bubble burst when the S & S man called and said that if I hadn't started the book they would publish the pieces I had been writing for *Saturday Review*. He said he hadn't read them, so I sent him a stack of columns.

A few days later I was called in to S & S. They hung my hat and coat, served me tea, and I began to feel like an author. He liked the pieces and they would be put into book form. My "thinking money" had evidently run out.

Before the book was published there appeared a small newspaper item that S & S was publishing a book by me. For the first time since our lunch I heard from the man at Doubleday. He was deeply hurt. I explained that this was a previous commitment and I would return his check. He was deeply hurt again and said they expected my next book to be sent to them.

A few days later I received a call from Simon & Schuster; it may have been a conference call. They said they were most enthused by my *Saturday Review* pieces and wanted me to write another book on any subject I chose. I asked if there was to be some "thinking money." They said of course. I asked how much.

They asked how much I wanted. I said two thousand dollars, and would they please send it to the man at Doubleday and leave me out as middleman. There was a long pause and they quietly hung up.

Now to prove how history has this miserable fault of repeating itself, last November out of a clear, blue, twelve-year-later sky I received a letter from Mr. Samuel Vaughan at Doubleday asking if I had ever considered writing a book. He had read a piece of mine which appeared in *Fortune* and he was inviting me to become a candidate for an advance check.

I wrote Mr. Vaughan, saying that evidently he was new around Doubleday because I had been on their books for two thousand dollars for some twelve years and owed him a book plus the interest. He investigated and phoned to say, "By George, you're right. How about writing the book now?" I replied I was ready to pay my debt to society. He suggested I use the *Fortune* magazine piece along with the columns written in this space. It was agreed.

Late that same afternoon I received a phone call from my man at the William Morris Agency. He said he had a call from a man at Simon & Schuster who had read the *Fortune* piece and wanted me to write a book. My man had agreed and they had already mailed me a check for three thousand dollars "thinking money." Well, here we go again.

Quickly I arranged for a meeting with the S & S man. My Morris Agency man asked, "What do you want the meeting for? Just write the book." I said I only wanted to explain something to him. "What's to explain? Just write the book." They all keep saying, "Just write the book."

The meeting took place the following day with S & S's Mr. Peter Schwed. I laid my cards on the table. What a messy deck that turned out to be. I told him the story of Doubleday twelve years ago, and since he was new there I brought him up to date on my last deal with S & S. "So you see," I concluded, "I have no integrity. I am not responsible. It'll be all I can do to write that book for Doubleday."

He skipped "no integrity" and "not responsible" and asked what the Doubleday book was about. I said it would contain the columns from *Saturday Review* and as a format it would feature several pieces I wrote on the art of living with hypochondria. It would point up humorously the sufferings of a hypochondriac and would be in the nature of a first-aid book for similar sufferers with kindred symptoms and perhaps allay their fears. I explained this was my metier because for years I had been a hypochondriac and I graphically detailed the afflictions that had beset me from head to toe.

Mr. Schwed patiently listened to my organ recital and by now I could see that to "hypochondria" he had secretly added "kleptomania." I offered to return the check. He recoiled in horror.

"Just write the book," he said. "Have you any other idea for a book?"

I said I had. I didn't know when I'd get around to

it but I'd always wanted to write an autobiographical book about all the interesting and exciting things that have happened with actors I've met in my writing life. I would call it *Capital I*. It would be a love story because everyone knows actors are in love with themselves.

He liked that. "Just write the book," he said.

And I will. Now all I have to do is wait around for something interesting and exciting to happen in my writing life.

Epilogue

On the last visit to the doctor's office for my annual checkup, which I take every week, he stood me on his scale again and angrily announced that I was not following the diet he had prescribed.

"You're still overweight," he shouted.

"I think you're wrong, doctor," I replied. "It's not my weight. According to this chart I am now at the correct weight for a man six feet, eight inches tall. It's my height that needs correcting."

He's working on it.

G. A.